The Distribution of the Tax Burden

The Distribution of the Tax Burden

Edgar K. Browning and
William R. Johnson

American Enterprise Institute for Public Policy Research
Washington, D.C.

Edgar K. Browning is professor of economics at the University of Virginia and an AEI adjunct scholar. William R. Johnson is associate professor of economics at the University of Virginia.

Library of Congress Cataloging in Publication Data

Browning, Edgar K
    The distribution of the tax burden.
      1. Tax incidence—United States. 2. Taxation,
Progressive. I. Johnson, William R., 1943-   joint
author. II. Title.
HJ2322.A3B76   336.2'94'0973   79-9489
ISBN 0-8447-3349-0

AEI Studies 246

The views expressed in the publications of the American Enterprise Institute are those of the authors and do not necessarily reflect the views of the staff, advisory panels, officers, or trustees of AEI.

"American Enterprise Institute" is the registered service mark of the American Enterprise Institute for Public Policy Research.

Printed in the United States of America

CONTENTS

List of Tables

List of Figures

1
Introduction and Summary

The way in which the total tax burden is distributed among households by the U.S. tax system is a topic of vital concern to policy makers. When President Carter referred to the tax system as a "national disgrace," he based his judgment in part on the widely accepted view that tax burdens are approximately proportional to household income. Despite the fact that the federal personal income tax structure is progressive, when social security, sales and excise, corporation, and property taxes are taken into account, the overall impact of the tax system is thought to be nearly proportional.[1] If this view is correct, then wealthy households do not pay a significantly larger share of their incomes in taxes (and actually may pay a smaller share according to some estimates) than low-income households. Several recent studies have lent empirical support to this view.[2] Many persons concerned with the equity of our tax system view such a distribution of tax burdens as being unfair. Most efforts to reform the tax system are based on such a view, seeking changes in the federal tax structure to make the overall tax system more progressive. As noted in one recent study, "imparting a more progres-

---

[1] A tax is proportional if the tax burden is the same percentage of before-tax income at all income levels; a tax is progressive if the tax burden is a larger percentage of before-tax income at higher income levels; a tax is regressive if the tax burden is a smaller percentage of before-tax income at higher income levels. Alternatively, this distinction can be made in terms of how the average tax rate varies with income; a tax is progressive if the average tax rate increases with income, regressive if the average tax rate falls as income rises, and proportional if the average tax rate is the same at all income levels.

[2] See, in particular, Joseph A. Pechman and Benjamin A. Okner, *Who Bears the Tax Burden?* (Washington, D.C.: Brookings Institution, 1974); and Richard A. Musgrave, Karl E. Case, and Herman Leonard, "The Distribution of Fiscal Burdens and Benefits," *Public Finance Quarterly*, vol. 2 (July 1974), pp. 259-311.

sive shape to the tax system by one means or another is the major thrust of most reforming efforts."[3]

This study develops new estimates of the distribution of federal, state, and local government taxes by income class for 1976. In contrast to previous studies, however, we find that the overall tax system is already highly progressive, with tax rates rising from 11.7 percent for the poorest 10 percent of households to 38.3 percent for the wealthiest 10 percent of households. The difference between these estimates and those presented in previous studies reflects largely a change in the theoretical analysis of the burden of indirect business taxes. Chapter 2 shows that the earlier studies have relied on a questionable theoretical analysis that has led to a substantial under-estimation of the degree of progressivity of the tax system.

Chapter 2 deals with tax incidence theory, that branch of economic theory dealing with the determination of who actually bears the burden of various taxes. It points out what we believe to be a theoretical error in previous studies and explains the appropriate treatment of the taxes in question. Chapter 3 explains the concept of household income used in this study and discusses the data employed in estimating tax burdens by income class. Chapter 4 presents and discusses the empirical results. The Appendix considers the quantitative significance of the incidence assumptions used in this study that differ from those of previous studies. In the remainder of this chapter, we will briefly discuss the theory, data, and major findings of the study.

Theory

To determine who bears the burden of any tax, a theory explaining how the economic system responds to the tax is necessary. In the next chapter, the rudiments of modern tax incidence theory that provide the basis for allocating tax burdens among households will be discussed. In common with other recent tax incidence studies, we adopt the approach that seems best justified by the accepted theory in this area. We differ only in the treatment of taxes levied on business output such as excise and sales taxes. This difference has important implications for the measured degree of progressivity of the tax system.

To illustrate, consider an excise tax applied to a product. Most analysts, as well as the general public, accept the view that an excise tax raises the price of the taxed product while leaving the prices of

---

[3] George F. Break and Joseph A. Pechman, *Federal Tax Reform* (Washington, D.C.: Brookings Institution, 1975), p. 11.

other products and factors of production (such as labor and capital) unchanged. Thus, it seems reasonable to assign the burden of such an excise tax to households in proportion to their consumption of the taxed product. This procedure, generally followed in tax incidence studies, has led to the belief that excise (and sales) taxes are regressive since low-income households devote a higher percentage of their incomes to consumption expenditures than do high-income families. Despite the plausibility of this position, we believe that it is correct only under extremely restrictive assumptions.

If an excise tax does in fact raise the price of the taxed product and leave other prices undisturbed, consider the effect upon a person whose entire income is a social security pension. If the size of his pension remains unchanged, he will bear a tax burden relative to his consumption of the taxed product. Under existing law, however, social security pensions are linked to the general price level (specifically, to the consumer price index). If the general level of prices rises, social security pensions automatically increase to keep the real purchasing power of the pensions unchanged. When the price of the taxed product increases, other prices remaining unchanged, the average level of prices rises, and social security pensions are increased accordingly. With a larger pension, the social security recipient bears no tax burden even though he continues to consume the higher priced product, unless he devotes a larger than average portion of his income to the taxed product.

A key element in this argument is that the source of a household's income has an important bearing on the extent to which the household bears a burden from a tax that falls on business output. Government transfer payments (such as social security pensions) are an important source of income for many households, and about three-fourths of all transfers are explicitly linked to the general price level or to the prices of specific products (for in-kind transfers such as Medicare). To the extent that transfers are indexed to prices, it is appropriate to assume that the real value of the transfers is unaffected by indirect business taxes. If this is so, then the burden of this type of tax should be assigned in proportion only to other types of income, such as labor and capital income, which will not rise automatically if a tax leads to higher prices of goods and services. Assigning a tax in proportion to factor income (labor plus capital income), however, implies that its burden is progressively distributed among income classes since factor income is a lower percentage of total income for low-income households who receive a larger percentage of their total incomes as government transfers. Allocating the burden of sales and excise taxes in proportion to factor income rather than to consumption is the major difference between this and other tax incidence studies.

The analysis here implies that sales and excise taxes are progressive elements in the tax system instead of regressive forces as they are conventionally labeled. The theoretical analysis supporting this conclusion is developed in greater detail in Chapter 2. That Chapter also considers the significance for tax incidence of differences in the proportion of income consumed among income classes. The quantitative significance of this issue is treated in the Appendix. In addition, Chapter 2 presents a methodological defense of the assumption that the real value of transfers is unchanged by indirect business taxes and shows how previous studies have been internally inconsistent because of a failure to treat transfers in this way.

Our analysis of sales and excise taxes also has important implications for the distributional effects of several other taxes under noncompetitive incidence assumptions. If it is assumed that the economic system functions in a competitive manner, economists are in general agreement about the distributional effects of corporation income taxes, property taxes, and the employer portion of social security taxes. Under competitive assumptions, it can be shown that corporate and property taxes are borne by recipients of capital income, and the employer portion of social security taxes is borne by workers in proportion to their covered earnings. Not all economists agree, however, that the U.S. economy is sufficiently competitive for these conclusions to hold in practice. Many analysts contend, for example, that corporations may simply raise the prices of their products in response to the corporation income tax, as if it were an excise tax instead of a tax on the return to capital in the corporate sector.

The lack of consensus about the degree of competition in the economy has led tax incidence analysts to employ a range of assumptions which reflect various possibilities. Previous studies suggest that under competitive incidence assumptions the tax system is mildly progressive while under certain noncompetitive assumptions the tax burden becomes approximately proportional to income. In other words, the more noncompetitive the economy is assumed to be, the less progressive the tax system is. This relationship results from reasoning similar to that employed in the analysis of sales and excise tax incidence: taxes collected from businesses (in a noncompetitive setting) lead to higher product prices. Subsequently, if the tax burden is allocated according to consumption, it will be regressively distributed among income classes, making the system less progressive than under competitive conditions.

Our analysis implies that this reasoning is also incorrect. If businesses respond in a noncompetitive fashion to, say, the corporation income tax and simply raise prices, then it is not appropriate to allocate the tax burden in proportion to consumption expenditures. Instead, the tax should be treated as if it were an excise or sales tax and allocated in proportion to factor income. This assignment leads to a significantly different distribution of the tax burden, as empirical results here will show.

Data

Technically, a tax incidence study involves two steps: the determination of the before-tax incomes of households and the assignment of tax burdens to these households.

In identifying the before-tax incomes of households, it is desirable to use a comprehensive measure of income so that the standard of living each household could attain (before taxes) is estimated accurately. The major statistical problem is that available data on the distribution of income do not measure income in a comprehensive way. Therefore, the figures were adjusted for the excluded items insofar as possible.

The data initially contained estimates of the distribution of money income among a representative sample of U.S. households collected by the U.S. Bureau of Census. Three major types of income (not received as cash) that were omitted in the Census Bureau's figures had to be imputed to the sample: in-kind government transfers (such as food stamps), imputed rental income of owner-occupied housing, and accrued capital gains.

The next adjustment made to the data involved converting household incomes to their before-tax equivalents. Incomes received by households are not equal to what their incomes would be in the absence of taxation because of taxes collected from businesses. A tax such as the corporation income tax, for instance, diverts funds to the government that would otherwise have gone to the owners of factors of production. Thus, indirect business taxes must be added to the incomes of households who would have received the funds in the absence of these taxes.

After these adjustments, our estimate of total before-tax (but after-transfer) household income in 1976 is $1,574.3 billion. In contrast, total money income received by households was $1,205 billion. This means that our before-tax income concept is, on average, about 30 percent larger than the figure most households consider their before-tax income.

Major Findings

Under competitive incidence assumptions, the distribution of tax burdens (as represented by effective tax rates on before-tax incomes) for 1976 is shown in Figure 1. Households have been ranked on the basis of their before-tax incomes and grouped into deciles, each containing 10 percent of all households. Figure 1 shows the average tax rate for each decile, that is, the total federal, state, and local tax burden for each decile divided by its total before-tax income.

As seen in Figure 1, under competitive assumptions the tax system is sharply progressive. Taxes are 11.7 percent of the total before-tax income of households in the lowest decile, and this fraction rises steadily until it reaches 38.3 percent for the highest decile. In absolute terms, the tax burden for the average household in the lowest decile is $353 while it is $24,624 for the average household in the highest decile. The average tax rate for all households (total taxes of $458 billion divided by total before-tax income of $1574 billion) is 29.1 percent. Only the top two deciles are subject to a tax rate that exceeds the national average figure. Households in these two deciles pay 57 percent of all taxes; households in the lowest two deciles pay less than 2 percent of all taxes.

The major reason tax rates are so low for households in the lower deciles of the before-tax income distribution is that these households receive a large fraction of their incomes in the form of non-taxed government transfers. Transfers account for 60 percent of total income for the bottom decile and 55 percent for the second decile. In contrast, transfers compose only 4 percent of the income of the top decile; most of the income of these households stems from payments to labor and capital which are subject to taxation.

Alternatively, Figure 2 displays average tax rates by decile for a specific set of noncompetitive incidence assumptions. In preparing these estimates, we have assumed that half of employer social security taxes, half of corporation income taxes, and half of property taxes are shifted in the same manner as sales or excise taxes. The tax system remains highly progressive under these conditions, with rates rising from 10.7 percent for the bottom decile to 36.4 percent for the top decile. Indeed, the distribution of tax burdens is almost identical to that found under the competitive assumptions: each decile's tax rate varies by less than two percentage points under the two sets of assumptions.

It should be mentioned that the noncompetitive incidence assumptions underlying Figure 2 tend to stand at the extreme non-

FIGURE 1

Average Tax Rates: Competitive Incidence Assumptions 1976

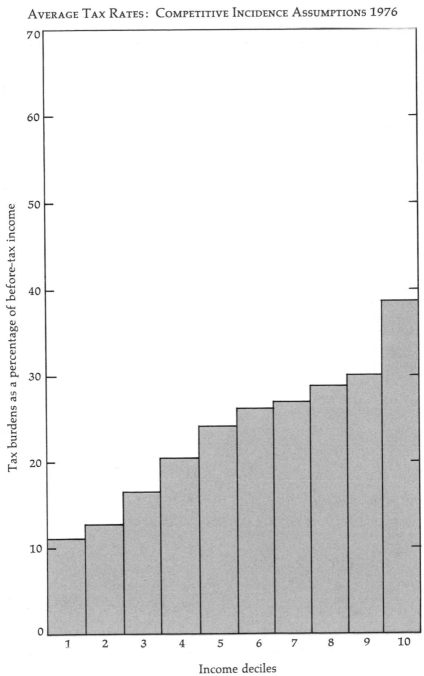

Income deciles

FIGURE 2

Average Tax Rates: Noncompetitive Incidence Assumptions

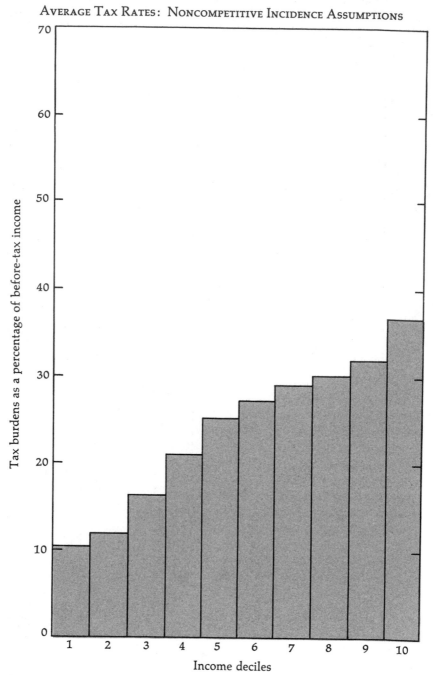

competitive end of the spectrum of incidence variants that have generally been employed. Thus, our finding that the degree of progressivity in the tax system is virtually unaffected by substituting noncompetitive assumptions for competitive assumptions suggests that the tax system is highly progressive regardless of the degree of competition in the economy, at least for the range of incidence assumptions that economists have found to be plausible.

A novel feature of this study is the estimation of marginal tax rates confronting households at different income levels. Marginal tax rates are those that apply to a change in income from a given level. Thus, if a household pays $40 in additional taxes when its earnings increase by $100, its marginal tax rate is 40 percent. The level of marginal tax rates is important because of its effect on productive incentives. The higher the marginal tax rate, the lower the incentive to increase earnings and the greater the incentive to reduce earnings, other things equal. Average tax rates, such as those shown in Figures 1 and 2, can also affect incentives, but their major usefulness in analysis lies in indicating the distributional effects of taxes.

A household's marginal tax rate is affected not only by taxes but also by any government transfers it receives. Many transfer programs tend to reduce the size of the payments when a household's earnings increase, and this action has the same effect upon productive incentives as taxing additional earnings. What is relevant to productive incentives is the effective marginal tax rate that results from the combined effect of taxes rising and transfers falling when earnings increase. Since our data base contains information on both taxes and transfers, we have been able to develop estimates of effective marginal tax rates by income class.

Figure 3 displays estimates of effective marginal tax rates by income class. In general, these rates are substantially higher than average tax rates and are the greatest for the lowest and highest income classes. The marginal tax rate for the bottom income class is the highest of all at 62.9 percent. Thus, if an average household in this income class increases its earnings by, say, $100, its disposable income would rise by only $37. Conversely, if earnings are reduced by $100, disposable income falls by only $37. The high marginal rates for the lower income classes are largely the result of transfers falling as earnings increase, while the rates for higher income classes (where transfers are relatively unimportant) are primarily the product of the tax system.

FIGURE 3

MARGINAL TAX RATES: COMPETITIVE INCIDENCE ASSUMPTIONS

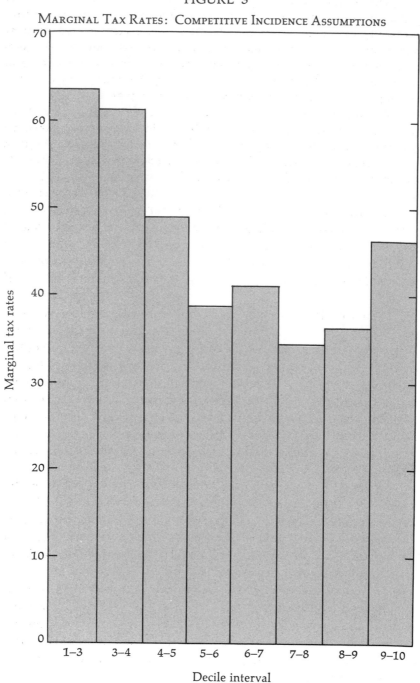

Approximately 50 percent of all households (the lowest 40 percent and highest 10 percent of income earners) are confronted with rates close to or exceeding 50 percent; marginal tax rates tend to be lowest for upper-middle income households. Over the entire range of incomes, the average marginal tax rate is 45.5 percent. In other words, if a household increases its earnings so that it moves from the lowest to the highest income class, its disposable income will rise by 54.5 percent of the increase in earnings while net government revenue (increased taxes plus reduced transfers) will rise by 45.5 percent of the increase in earnings.

All of these estimates pertain to the tax and transfer programs in effect in 1976. The major change in government policy since 1976 that is relevant for these estimates is the increase in social security taxes enacted late in 1977. This change, composed of a small increase in the tax rate and a large increase in the ceiling on taxable earnings, is being phased in over several years. If the new tax law was fully in effect in 1976, the major impact would be to increase marginal and average tax rates on individual earnings above the 1976 ceiling on taxable earnings ($15,300). The exact magnitude of these increases is not clear at this time. (A more complete discussion of these and other results is presented in Chapter 4.)

2
Tax Incidence Theory

This chapter develops the economic analysis underlying the assignment of tax burdens to households. We will begin by discussing some general elements of tax incidence theory[1] and then turn to an examination of the major taxes in the tax system. While this analysis is necessarily somewhat abstract, a background in the theoretical basis of the rules used to allocate the burden of taxes to households is fundamental to an understanding of the distribution of the tax burden.

Elements of Tax Incidence Analysis

Nature of Tax Incidence. The economic agent legally responsible for transferring tax funds to the government may not actually bear the final burden of the tax. For example, the owner of a business whose product is subject to an excise or sales tax probably does not bear the burden of the tax despite the fact that he writes the check to the government to cover the tax liability. If this is so, who does bear the burden? Answering this question for various types of taxes is the major objective of tax incidence analysis. Clearly, assignment of the burden depends on the way in which a tax affects the price of the taxed product as well as other prices (including prices of factors of

---

[1] For general discussions of tax incidence theory in a general equilibrium context, see Richard A. Musgrave, *The Theory of Public Finance* (New York: McGraw-Hill, 1959), ch. 10; Peter M. Mieszkowski, "On the Theory of Tax Incidence," *Journal of Political Economy*, vol. 75 (June 1967), pp. 250-262, and "Tax Incidence Theory: The Effects of Taxes on the Distribution of Income," *Journal of Economic Literature*, vol. 7 (December 1969), pp. 1103-1124; Charles E. McLure, Jr., "General Equilibrium Incidence Analysis: The Harberger Model after Ten Years," *Journal of Public Economics*, vol. 4 (February 1975), pp. 125-161; and George F. Break, "The Incidence and Economic Effects of Taxation," in *The Economics of Public Finance* (Washington, D.C.: Brookings Institution, 1974), pp. 119-237.

production). Much of tax incidence analysis involves determining how a tax, by changing the economic incentives confronting firms and individuals, will lead to alterations in the prices of products and factors of production.

One of the conceptual problems in determining tax incidence is how to account for the government's use of the tax revenues. Any analysis that ignored the way tax revenues were used would be seriously incomplete. Tax specialists generally employ one of two approaches. In the first, balanced-budget incidence, the tax revenue is assumed to be spent by government in some specific way, say, by purchasing airplanes. The incidence of the tax is reflected in the way the joint tax-expenditure operation affects the disposable income of all households. On average, of course, disposable income falls by the amount of tax revenue collected, but individual households are likely to be affected in ways that differ from the average effect.

The second approach is called differential incidence. In this approach, it is assumed that the tax to be analyzed is substituted for some other tax, while total tax revenue and government expenditures remain unchanged. Since total revenue and expenditures are fixed, there is no net reduction in the disposable incomes of the public. Nonetheless, there is likely to be a change in the distribution of disposable income among households: some will bear a heavier tax burden than before the tax substitution and others a lighter burden.

Both of these approaches take explicit account of the use of tax revenues; in one case the tax finances some expenditure, and in the other it permits a reduction in the reliance on some other tax. Neither of these approaches, however, is without ambiguity. In the case of balanced-budget incidence, the expenditure of the tax revenues by the government must be specified since the final effect on disposable income can depend on how the funds are actually spent. Unfortunately, it is frequently impossible to determine the specific expenditure programs financed by a given tax. Alternatively, in the case of differential incidence, some tax must be specified as a benchmark against which all other taxes are compared. Generally, a proportional tax on all income serves this function. Then the differential incidence of, say, a sales tax involves determining how the distribution of disposable income would be affected if a sales tax were substituted for a proportional income tax of equal yield.

These approaches represent two different ways of carefully taking into account the way in which tax revenues are used. Choosing between them depends in part on the issues being analyzed. For example, if the issue is tax reform, differential incidence becomes the logical approach since the object is to change the tax system without increasing or reducing total revenues. Alternatively, if the question is the way in which the cost of supporting existing government expenditures is apportioned among the public, then balanced-budget incidence is the logical approach.

The analysis in this study utilizes the balanced-budget approach. This choice necessitates incorporating expenditure effects into the analysis. Since determining actual expenditures financed by given taxes is impossible as a practical matter, we assume that expenditures are, on the average, "distributionally neutral," in the jargon of tax analysts. Roughly, this means that the distributional impact of government expenditures (their effect on product and factor prices) is no different than if the revenues were returned to households to be spent as they wish.[2] This assumption will obviously not be correct in all cases, but it permits attention to be focused on the effects of taxes on product and factor prices in the simplest way. At the present time, we have little evidence indicating the direction or magnitude of effects produced by actual government expenditures which deviate from being distributionally neutral.

Many tax analysts prefer the use of differential incidence analysis because it avoids the necessity of making the strong assumption that expenditures are distributionally neutral. We adopt the balanced-budget approach mainly for ease of exposition in the analysis; actually, there is little substantive difference between the two approaches when the distributional neutrality assumption is made in balanced-budget analysis.[3] Balanced-budget incidence re-

---

[2] For the case of an economy producing two goods, x and y, McLure explains distributional neutrality more carefully as the condition "that all individuals and the government have the same marginal propensity to consume good x and the same income-compensated elasticity of demand for good x with respect to relative product prices P_x/P_y, but that individuals do not necessarily have the same average propensity to consume good x." See Charles E. McLure, Jr., "Tax Incidence, Macroeconomic Policy, and Absolute Prices," Quarterly Journal of Economics, vol. 82 (May 1969), p. 255. As stated, this assumption may appear more restrictive than is actually necessary. It is not necessary that the government purchase exactly the same goods as individuals; it could simply employ the same factors of production that would have been used to produce the goods consumers would have bought. Thus, the fact that government purchases national defense services, which consumers would not have bought on their own, does not necessarily invalidate the distributional neutrality assumption.

[3] As Mieszkowski points out: "In practice, however, the difference between the two approaches is minor as most results on differential incidence can easily be translated into absolute burdens by using the proportional income tax as a 'reference point'." See Mieszkowski, "Tax Incidence Theory," p. 1105. Some economists, however, have been very critical of the balanced-budget approach because of the apparent restrictiveness of the assumption of distributional

sults derived with this assumption can easily be translated into differential incidence. For example, suppose the balanced-budget approach implies that a particular income class bears a 4 percent burden under a sales tax and a 5 percent burden under a proportional income tax of equal yield. This analysis implies that if the sales tax is substituted for the income tax, this income class will derive a gain equal to 1 percent of its income, the difference between the 4 and 5 percent burdens. Some readers may prefer to interpret the results in terms of differential incidence.

Tax Effects on Sources and Uses of Income. Our object is to determine how a tax affects a person's real disposable income.[4] In general, there are two different ways in which real incomes may be affected by a tax: on the sources of income side of the budget or on the uses of income side.

Sources of income. A tax may reduce the income that is available to be spent. If the tax reduces a household's income from $10,000 to $9,000, the tax is said to place a burden on the sources of income side of the household's budget. Income derives from one of three sources: payment for labor services rendered (labor income); payment for capital services rendered (capital income); and unrequited transfers from the government (transfer income). If a tax reduces the net payment received from any, or all, of these sources, it is said to place a burden on the sources side of the budget. It is important to recognize that a burden can occur on the sources side in two distinct ways. One is familiar: after a household receives its income, part of it must be turned over to the government. Personal income taxes (outside of the part withheld) are paid in this way. The sources side is affected in another way when the tax is collected before the person receives the income. Suppose the employer pays a payroll tax (social security, for example) on the wages of workers. If he reduces wage rates in response to the tax, the workers bear a burden on the sources side in the form of a lower wage rate received from the employer. In both these cases, the effect is to reduce the net (after-tax) wage rate and thereby to leave the household with a smaller disposable income.

---

neutrality for government expenditures. See, for example, Break, "The Incidence and Economic Effects of Taxation," p. 128.

[4] The analysis developed in the next several pages is based on Edgar K. Browning, "The Burden of Taxation," *Journal of Political Economy*, vol. 86 (August 1978), pp. 649-671.

Uses of income. A tax can also affect real disposable income by causing a change in the prices of goods that are purchased with the income. Even if a person's money income is unchanged by a tax, if the relative prices of goods he consumes heavily increase, then the purchasing power of his income is reduced. In this case, the tax is said to place a burden on the uses side of the household budget since the burden results from the use of income to purchase higher priced products.

Much of modern tax incidence analysis is devoted to determining how taxes affect the sources or uses of income, or both. The total tax burden on any household is the sum of these two different effects. Not all taxes will affect both sources and uses; some may affect only one side of the budget. It is generally believed, for example, that the federal personal income tax has little or no effect on the prices of goods and services; instead, it merely reduces disposable income on the sources side. If this is correct, then the personal income tax places a burden only on the sources side. By contrast, some observers argue that an excise tax puts a burden only on the uses side, raising the price of the taxed product, but leaving other prices (including wage rates) unchanged. (As will be shown later, this assessment is probably not fully accurate.) Other taxes can affect both the uses and sources sides of income. In all cases, care must be taken to determine whether a tax affects households in one or both of these two ways before attempting to measure the burden.

Absolute and Relative Prices. In discussing taxes, it is important to distinguish between absolute and relative price changes. An absolute price change refers to the movement in price, measured in dollars, of a given product, taken alone. If the price of a product, x, rises from $1.00 to $1.10, then its absolute price has risen by 10 percent. Whether this represents a change in the relative price of x depends on the behavior of other prices. If all other prices, including those of the factors of production, have also risen by 10 percent, relative prices have not changed. Every product and factor of production still costs the same relative to others as before the price increase. If, on the other hand, no other prices change when the price of x rises from $1.00 to $1.10, then the price of x has risen both absolutely and relative to other goods and services. Moreover, in this case the absolute price level, the average prices of goods and services, has also increased since one price has risen and no other price has fallen.

There is wide agreement among economists that most taxes affect the relative prices of goods and services. The effect of taxes on the absolute price level is not as clear. Does a general sales tax cause the prices of all goods and services to rise, thereby increasing the absolute price level? It can be argued that a sales tax has no effect on absolute product prices. Aggregate demand for goods and services is not in any obvious way increased by the imposition of a tax: private demand for goods and services falls when taxes are collected, but this decrease is offset when the government spends the revenue. Alternatively, however, it can be argued that in some way the overall price level would be higher if a general sales tax were imposed. Given the many factors that influence the overall price level, this latter possibility cannot be ruled out.

What really matters here is the relationship of the tax burden to increases in the price level. In recent years, tax specialists have argued that the movement of the absolute price level has no effect on the distribution of real tax burdens. Consider a general sales tax again. If the price level is unaffected by the imposition of a sales tax, firms will receive unchanged receipts from the sale of their products. Since some portion of these receipts must be turned over to the government, firms will have fewer funds than before to pay factors of production. Consequently, demand for the factors of production will fall, and wage rates and other factor prices will go down. In this case, the tax burden falls on the sources side because capital and labor income fall while product prices remain unchanged.

Alternatively, suppose the absolute price level rises in proportion to the sales tax, and there is no change in the prices of the factors of production. In this case, the burden of the tax appears to fall on the uses side of the budget since product prices rise, and there is no effect on the sources side. Actually, the real effects may be the same in these two cases. In both situations, prices of the factors of production (that is, factor incomes) have fallen relative to product prices. In the first case, product prices were unchanged and wages rates (and other factor prices) fell so that workers' real earnings were lower after the tax. In the second case, product prices rose and wage rates were unchanged; once again the real wage rate (the money wage rate expressed in dollars of constant purchasing power) has fallen. In both these cases, the burden is really on the sources side: the purchasing power of the income received by factors of production is reduced by the tax.[5]

---

[5] The sources-side effects of taxes refer to changes in the real purchasing power of disposable income, which depends on how factor prices change relative to the average level of product prices. A rise in nominal product prices with unchanged nominal factor prices is a relative decline in factor prices and is a burden on

Using similar reasoning, it has been shown that under certain conditions the real effects of a tax remain the same regardless of what happens to the absolute price level.[6] The determining factor is the effect of the tax on relative prices. In both cases analyzed above, prices of the factors of production, such as wage rates, fell relative to product prices, and this change in relative prices determines the distribution of the real tax burden.

There is, however, a problem with this argument. It is valid only for an economy in which households' entire incomes are in the form of payments for supplying factors of production, that is, labor and capital income. In the U.S. economy, however, government transfers are a third important source of income. The validity of the argument must be reevaluated for the situation where some households receive government transfers. Consider a household whose entire income consists of government transfer payments. Clearly the household's real economic position may depend on what happens to the price level. If the transfer is fixed in money terms and the price level remains unchanged in response to the imposition of a sales tax, then the household bears no burden. On the other hand, if the price level rises, the purchasing power of an unchanged money transfer falls, and the tax places a burden on the household. Consequently, in the case of government transfers the incidence of taxes may not be independent of absolute price level effects after all.

Previous tax incidence studies have allocated the burden of the sales tax in proportion to consumption outlays. Insofar as transfer receipts are concerned, this allocation would be correct if the sales tax increases the price level exactly in proportion to the size of the tax and if the money value of the transfer were fixed. Under these conditions, transfer recipients would bear the estimated burden under the sales tax. These conditions, however, are highly restrictive, and it is worthwhile considering whether they are plausible.

At least two major problems arise in allocating the tax burden of a sales tax in proportion to consumption outlays for transfer recipients. First, this approach necessarily assumes that the price level will rise exactly in proportion to the size of the tax (tax revenue as a percentage of national income). If the sales tax generates revenues equal to 5 percent of national income, then all product prices must be

the sources side, not on the uses side despite the fact that the nominal level of product prices has risen. A uses-side effect is produced by a change in the *relative* prices of products purchased.

[6] See Musgrave, *The Theory of Public Finance*, pp. 364-371; and McLure, "Tax Incidence." These studies recognize that the conclusion must be qualified to the extent that people have assets fixed in money terms.

assumed to rise by 5 percent as a result of the tax. This increase would reduce the purchasing power of a given money transfer by about 5 percent. The problem with this assumption is that while economists may not agree on whether a sales tax leads to some increase in prices, there is certainly no basis for believing that the increase will be exactly proportionate to the amount of tax revenue.

A second problem with this approach concerns the assumption that the money value of the transfers remains fixed when the price level rises.[7] Actually, money values of many important government transfers are explicitly linked to changes in the price level. Social security, the single most important transfer program, is an example. Social security benefits are tied to the consumer price index through existing legislation. If the federal government enacted a value added tax which resulted in a 10 percent increase in the price level, social security benefits would also rise 10 percent automatically. For social security beneficiaries, the real purchasing power of their transfers is independent of the price level.

A number of other transfer programs are similar. Subsidies under the food stamp program are linked to the consumer price index. In-kind transfers, by their very nature, are related to the absolute prices of the subsidized goods. A recipient of Medicaid benefits, for example, is not harmed if the price of medical services rises since the government covers these costs.

The money value of approximately three-fourths of all government transfers will rise automatically if the price level rises. Transfers not automatically indexed to the price level may also rise, however, since legislatures are likely to increase transfers when an increase in the price level occurs. Legislatures are quite aware that the poverty levels of income rise when prices increase and may tend to respond by raising the money value of transfers to keep recipients from falling behind. Studies showing how transfers have varied during inflationary periods generally support the view that transfers will rise at least as fast as the price level.[8]

In view of these considerations, we believe the most reasonable assumption to employ in tax incidence analysis is that the real value

[7] A higher price level and unchanged transfer in money terms implies a lower transfer in real terms. An alternative assumption, which would have the same result, is that the real value of all transfers falls exactly in proportion to the size of the tax (tax revenue as a percentage of national income). For much the same reason as explained in the text, this assumption also appears implausible.

[8] John L. Palmer, "Inflation, Unemployment and Poverty" (Ph.D. dissertation, Stanford University, 1971), ch. 9. See also Joseph J. Minarik, "Who Wins, Who Loses from Inflation?", The Brookings Bulletin, vol. 15 (Summer 1978), pp. 6-10.

or purchasing power of government transfers is unaffected by tax policy. This assumption implies, of course, that if the price level or the prices of goods subsidized with in-kind transfers rises, then government transfers will be increased in proportion. While this strict relationship probably does not apply in every instance, it appears to be a more plausible assumption than that implicitly underlying previous studies. Moreover, this assumption has the important advantage of implying that the distribution of real tax burdens does not depend on whether taxes affect the absolute price level. Consequently our conclusions are valid even if some taxes lead to a higher overall price level. (A further discussion of this important issue is contained in the last section of this chapter.)

For simplicity of exposition, it will be assumed that the absolute price level is unaffected by taxes. This assumption does not rule out the possibility that taxes may increase the relative prices of some goods and services. It does mean, however, that if a tax increases the dollar prices of some goods, the dollar prices of other goods must fall to maintain an unchanged overall price level. The process by which some taxes produce this effect will be examined when we consider the major taxes separately.

Burdens and Benefits on the Uses Side. As pointed out earlier, a tax may affect the real disposable income of households through changes in the sources or in the uses sides of household budgets, or both. Under the assumption of an unchanged absolute price level, tax effects on the uses side involve changes in the relative prices of goods and services. We will now show in some detail how changes in relative prices can involve both burdens and benefits for different households.

Consider a simple economy in which only two goods, x and y, are produced. Suppose that a tax is levied on good x. The result will be a higher relative price for good x, but since the overall price level is unchanged, this means a lower price for good y. More specifically, suppose that the price of good x rises by 10 percent and the price of good y falls by 10 percent. If the entire community devotes half its income to the purchase of each good, the overall price level will remain unchanged: half of outlays are made on a product 10 percent more expensive while half are made on a product 10 percent cheaper.

How this change in relative product prices (changes on the uses side of household budgets) affects individual households depends on the proportion of their incomes devoted to the two goods. For any household that spends half its income on each good, there is a zero net burden on the uses side. (There will, of course, be positive burdens on the sources side, but here only effects on the uses side are under consideration.) This household would gain as much from its purchases of the lower priced good as it would lose from the purchases of the higher priced good. Note that there is a zero net burden for the community as a whole on the uses side since half of total income is devoted to each good. The aggregate effect of any tax on the uses side of household budgets is always zero.[9]

Individual households, however, may be either burdened or benefited by the change in relative prices. If a household consumes only good x, whose price rises by 10 percent, it is obviously worse off. A household which consumes only good y would benefit from the effect of this tax on relative prices. In general, whether a household is harmed or benefited depends on how its consumption pattern deviates from the community average. Any household that devotes more than half its income to purchases of good x will be worse off on balance, while households that devote less than half their income to good x (more than half to y) will be better off.

The burden or benefit can be expressed as a proportion of income by applying the formula $[a_i P_x^* + (1 - a_i)P_y^*]$ where a_i is the proportion of income devoted to good x, $(1 - a_i)$ the proportion devoted to good y, P_x^* is the fractional change in the price of good x, and P_y^* is the fractional change in the price of good y. For a household that devotes half its income to each good, the formula gives $[0.5 (0.1) + 0.5 (-0.1)]$, or zero, as the net effect.[10] For a household spending 55 percent of its income on good x, the formula gives $[0.55 (0.1) + 0.45 (-0.1)]$, or 0.01, as the net effect. The burden on the uses side is equal to 1 percent of the household's income, analogous to a tax rate of 1 percent. Of course, if some households spend more than the national average on the taxed good, there must be others spending less who are benefited on the uses side.

---

[9] This is obvious from the assumption of an unchanged absolute price level, but it is also true if the price level varies. If all product prices rise, then payments to factors of production must be computed in dollars of constant purchasing power, implying a reduction in real incomes on the sources side. There would still be no net burden on the uses side.

[10] This exposition ignores the extent to which a change in relative prices caused by taxes may distort consumer choices. Most, if not all, taxes impose a burden in addition to that associated with the tax revenue itself by leading people to reallocate resources in an attempt to reduce their tax burden. In common with other studies of tax incidence, we are ignoring these excess burdens of taxation since they are difficult to measure and it is not clear how they would be distributed by income class. Most empirical studies have estimated that the excess burdens of taxes are generally less than 10 percent as large as the direct burdens that are measured in tax incidence studies.

It is important to note that the burden or benefit, expressed as a tax rate from the uses side, will be relatively small unless a household spends a percentage of its income on the taxed good that greatly deviates from the national average. In terms of the figures above, a household spending 60 percent of its income on good x (a proportion 20 percent higher than the national average of 50 percent) bears a burden of 2 percent. Of course, referring to this burden as a "small" effect implies some basis for comparison. In the example above, an excise tax on good x that would produce the specified change in prices would generate revenues equal to 10 percent of national income. Thus, the average burden of all households is 10 percent. (As will be shown below, this burden is assigned on the sources side.) Any additional effect on specific households from the uses side should be compared with the average burden of 10 percent in judging its significance.

In most cases, it seems clear that effects on households stemming from changes in relative prices will be small in comparison with the average burden of the tax. This is important to understand because it is one reason this study ignores these effects in estimating tax burdens by income class. In contrast to all previous studies of tax incidence, which have allocated certain taxes according to households' consumption of specific goods, this study allocates all taxes on the sources side of household budgets. There are compelling reasons for believing that this procedure produces more accurate estimates of tax burdens by income classes. Application of the theoretical framework to empirical evidence suggests that neglecting these relative price effects is unlikely to bias the results substantially.

As explained earlier, net burdens or benefits from changes in relative product prices arise only for households whose consumption patterns deviate from the national average. Since the concern here is with tax incidence by income class, the relevant question is how consumption patterns differ by income class. Table 1 provides information pertaining to this question. Consider first the percentages of household budgets devoted to alcohol, tobacco, and gasoline. These three goods are subject to heavy excise taxes, and there is little doubt that their relative prices are higher because of these taxes. As a national average, 7.2 percent of consumption outlays are devoted to these three goods. Households with an annual income of less than $3,000 spend 6.4 percent of their income on these goods. These households would gain from an increase in the relative price of taxed goods since they spend a smaller percentage of income on them than the national average. By contrast, the $7,000–7,999 income class

TABLE 1

Percentage of Consumption Outlays Expended on Selected Goods by Selected Income Classes, 1973
(percent)

Consumer Good	All Classes	Income Class			
		Less than $3,000	$7–7,999	$12–14,999	$25,000 or more
Alcohol	1.0	0.7	1.1	0.9	1.1
Tobacco	1.6	2.1	1.9	1.8	0.9
Gasoline	4.6	3.6	4.8	5.3	3.7
Food	19.5	21.9	20.8	20.0	16.4
Housing	30.5	38.9	31.7	29.5	28.9
Health care	6.1	6.7	6.8	5.8	5.5
Clothing	8.2	6.5	8.0	7.9	9.7
Recreation	8.2	5.2	6.0	7.8	11.3

Source: U.S. Department of Labor, Bureau of Labor Statistics, *Average Annual Expenditures for Commodity and Service Groups Classified by Nine Family Characteristics, 1972 and 1973*, Consumer Expenditure Survey Series: Interview Survey, 1972 and 1973, Report 455-3, 1976, table 1b.

devotes 7.8 percent of income to these goods, higher than the national average, so that this class would be harmed. However, the deviation from the national average is around 20 percent or less for every income class. These small deviations suggest that the size of the burden or benefit will be small, as illustrated by the earlier numerical example.

Even though these burdens and benefits will be small, there would be reason to include them if they could be calculated accurately. However, this calculation would require knowledge of the manner in which the prices of all goods and services are affected by the entire tax system. Excise taxes, of course, are not the only taxes that affect relative prices. Sales taxes, for example, frequently exempt certain goods such as food or health care and therefore tend to affect relative prices. Corporation income taxes, since they apply only to incorporated businesses, tend to raise the price of corporate products and reduce the prices of noncorporate products. Even income and payroll taxes can affect relative prices because of various exclusions and deductions in the tax base. The relevant information needed is the combined effect of all these taxes on the prices of all goods and services, but this cannot be determined with any accuracy.

Ignorance of the precise manner in which relative product prices are affected by the entire tax system would be a serious problem if consumption patterns differed greatly among income classes. If, however, consumption patterns are similar, only a minor problem exists: recall that if each income class devotes the same percentage of its budget to all goods, there is a zero net tax burden from the uses side regardless of how relative prices are affected. As Table 1 indicates, consumption patterns are fairly similar across income classes. In very few cases does any income class devote a proportion of total outlays to any good that deviates by more than 20 percent from the national average; in most cases, the deviation is smaller. Since deviations from the national average of this size imply only small burdens or benefits on the uses side, neglect of relative price effects should not bias the results to any significant degree.

Consumption-Saving Differences. So far this discussion has concentrated on the significance of differences in the patterns of consumption outlays. It is also important to consider the relevance of differences in the percentage of income consumed. There are substantial variations in the proportion of income that is devoted to consumption among income classes. For example, consumption expenditures by families with incomes in the lowest decile averaged 148 percent of their after-tax income, while the national average was 86.6 percent.[11]

In terms of the uses side of household budgets, income can be devoted to either consumption or saving, but taxes may alter the relative prices of these two ways of allocating income. (The "price" of saving is the inverse of the net interest rate received: the lower the interest rate, the more expensive it is to accumulate funds for future consumption.) A tax that falls on some or all consumer goods will then increase the price of consumption relative to saving. Whether or not this places a net burden on a household depends on the proportion of income saved. There would be a zero net effect for a household that saved the same percentage of its income as the national average. Since lower income households consume a substantially larger proportion of their income, however, the tax may impose a nontrivial burden on the uses side of budgets for this group.

The regressivity of the incidence of excise and sales taxes found in previous studies largely reflects this systematic difference in consumption relative to income. Since consumption is higher relative to income at low income levels, any tax allocated according to consumption will be regressive with respect to income.

---

[11] See the Appendix to this study for the source of these figures.

Allocating any tax in proportion to consumption outlays is not generally correct in principle; the preferable approach would be to estimate separately the tax effects on sources and uses of income and then sum them for each income class. However, another issue is relevant here. The accounting period used in measuring income and consumption is normally one year, primarily reflecting the way government statistics are collected. Using annual data imparts a systematic bias to consumption-income statistics because many people in the lowest income classes are there only for a short time. A person, for example, may become unemployed or ill and temporarily drop into a lower than normal income class. When this happens, his consumption will generally be more closely related to his normal income than to his temporarily depressed income. In short, he is likely to dissave (consume more than his current income) rather than live within his temporarily low income.[12]

The issue here is whether current consumption behavior based on the one-year accounting period or consumption behavior as related to longer-run circumstances is the relevant concept for tax analysis. Existing evidence suggests that differences in consumption-to-income ratios for low- and higher-income families are much smaller, if not negligible, when longer time periods are considered. Thus, the fact that families who have low income in a given year consume more than their incomes does not mean that they normally do so. In our view, it is the relationship between consumption and income for longer periods than a year that is relevant. Annual statistics can sometimes be misleading, as is the case with the consumption-to-income ratio. As Henry J. Aaron has noted, "prevailing evidence suggests that the difference between the consumption-income ratios of high- and low-income families is negligible if normal income is used."[13] This observation implies that any burdens or benefits on the uses side derived from differences in consumption-income ratios are also negligible if normal income is considered.

Some economists have argued that tax incidence studies should be based on annual incomes instead of normal incomes. Since the

---

[12] The fact that many low-income families have only temporarily low incomes also may have an effect on the composition of consumption outlays, as measured in Table 1. For example, it seems likely that families with normal incomes of less than $3,000 probably do not devote 38.9 percent of their outlays to housing. This unusually large fraction probably reflects the fact that housing outlays are related to normal incomes, and when incomes are temporarily low, these outlays are high in comparison with annual income.

[13] Henry J. Aaron, *Who Pays the Property Tax?* (Washington, D.C.: Brookings Institution, 1975), p. 30.

available statistics give estimates of annual incomes, there is little choice but to rely on these data. However, since annual statistics are known to misrepresent the behavior of persons typically in a certain income class, as is true of consumption-income ratios, it appears preferable to adopt a procedure that will measure how persons normally in that income class will be affected. (It should be noted that this issue is of little consequence for many taxes. Under personal income or payroll taxes, for example, a person with a temporarily low income will pay about the same tax as a person with a permanently low income so the tax burdens estimated using annual data will not be biased.)

Even if it is accepted that consumption-income ratios based on annual statistics are relevant for tax incidence studies, however, a further difficulty exists. Economists taking this position have argued that sales and excise taxes harm those who consume an above-average proportion of their income on the uses side and benefit those who save an above-average proportion. This analysis is correct for sales and excise taxes, but other taxes have opposing effects on the uses side of budgets that have not been evaluated in this way. In particular, corporation income taxes and property taxes reduce the net interest rate that savers receive. Consequently, these taxes harm savers and benefit consumers on the uses side in a way exactly opposite to sales and excise taxes. These effects, however, have not been incorporated into incidence studies. The relevant issue, as before, is the effect of the entire tax system on the prices of consumption goods relative to saving. Since sales and excise tax revenues are 8.1 percent of total consumption, while corporate and property tax revenues are 38.9 percent of before-tax capital income, the entire tax system probably changes relative prices in favor of consumption and against saving. Thus, if the annual consumption-income statistics were employed to make uses-side adjustments, low-income households would receive net benefits on the uses side while higher-income households would bear net losses.

If, however, consumption-income ratios do not differ among income classes, there is a zero net effect on the uses side, both for each tax considered separately as well as for the tax system as a whole. In this event, all taxes can be allocated accurately on the sources side of budgets. Since it is generally acknowledged that consumption-income ratios differ, at most, only slightly when consumption out of normal income is considered, the uses-side adjustments are small enough to neglect. Consequently, in this study all taxes are allocated on the sources side of household budgets.

To sum up this preliminary discussion briefly, two significant differences in tax incidence analysis are incorporated into this study. First, it is assumed that the real value of government transfers is unaffected by changes in tax policy. The practical reasons supporting this assumption relate to explicit and implicit indexing of transfers to the price level. A methodological defense of this assumption is presented in the last section of this chapter. Second, it is assumed that since consumption-income ratios do not differ greatly among income classes when consumption out of permanent income is considered, any uses-side effects will be small enough to neglect. Thus, all taxes can be allocated on the sources side. The quantitative significance of these two issues is examined in more detail in the Appendix to this study.

Analysis of Specific Taxes

An examination of the major taxes in the U.S. tax system illustrates the theoretical basis for the allocation of tax burdens by income class. It will be assumed, initially, that all markets are perfectly competitive and full employment prevails. In addition, the total supplies of labor and of saving are assumed to be unaffected by any tax.[14]

Sales and Excise Taxes. A general sales tax applies at equal rates to all consumer goods and services. Insofar as the tax applies to all goods and services, it has no effect on the relative prices of these final products. Under the assumption here that the absolute price level is unaffected, the absolute prices of products also remain unchanged. Firms find that they receive the same prices as before the tax, but now part of their receipts must be turned over to the government, leaving firms with lower net revenues to pay factors of production. Since the tax does not create any incentive for firms to alter the proportion in which they use factors of production, there will be a proportionate reduction in the price of all factors of production. (A proportionate reduction means that if the sales tax generates revenues equal to 2 percent of national income, factor prices will fall by 2 percent.) The incidence of the tax then falls on those who supply labor and capital services, and it falls in proportion to labor and capital income received.

---

[14] For a simplified exposition of the general equilibrium model underlying this analysis, see Charles E. McLure, Jr., and Wayne R. Thirsk, "A Simplified Exposition of the Harberger Model I: Tax Incidence," *National Tax Journal*, vol. 28 (March 1975), pp. 1-28. For a survey of the empirical evidence concerning the effect of taxes on labor supply and saving, see Break, "The Incidence and Economic Effects of Taxation."

Several points made earlier bear repeating here. First, the tax does not fall directly on consumers. Since all households are assumed to consume the same proportion of their incomes, there is no net effect on the uses side. Second, a household that receives no factor income bears no tax burden. Thus, the recipient of a government transfer bears no burden; he receives the same transfer and pays the same prices for goods and services as before. Third, these conclusions hold, even if the price level rises as a result of the sales tax, if the government increases the size of the transfer to maintain real purchasing power—an action which occurs through explicit and implicit indexing of transfers to the price level.

As developed, this analysis applies only to a national sales tax. In the United States, of course, sales taxes are used exclusively by state and local governments. If all states employed sales taxes at the same rate, the preceding analysis would require no qualification. However, not all states use sales taxes, and those that do employ varying rates. Since we intend to allocate sales taxes in proportion to factor income, irrespective of residence, we will overestimate the burden on people residing in states with lower than average sales taxes and underestimate the burden on those with higher than average sales taxes. Since the broad income classes being considered contain residents in all states, to some degree these underestimates and overestimates should balance out. Nonetheless, the estimation of tax burdens associated with state and local taxes generally must be understood to reflect the average burdens of these taxes across all states and localities.

In contrast to a sales tax, an excise tax is levied on the product of only one industry. Because the tax applies to just one product, the costs of producing that product rise relative to the costs of producing nontaxed products. This leads to a higher price and lower output of the taxed good. As output is restricted, some factors of production formerly employed to produce the taxed good must find employment in the production of nontaxed goods. A net increase in employment in the nontaxed sector will occur only if the prices of factors of production fall. As factor prices fall, costs of production in the nontaxed sector are reduced and the prices of those products also fall (otherwise consumers would not purchase the extra output). Moreover, factor prices fall somewhat in the taxed sector since the rate of pay for similar factors of production will be the same in all industries under competition.

To sum up: in the case of an excise tax, the price of the taxed product rises and the prices of other products, on the average, fall.

There is no net burden on the uses of income side of household budgets insofar as households devote the same percentage of income to the taxed product. The burden is on the sources side and is reflected in the lower factor prices received by suppliers of labor and capital. Under reasonable assumptions, labor and capital income will fall in the same proportion.[15] Therefore, the burden of an excise tax can be allocated in proportion to labor and capital income.

At the risk of needless repetition, it may be explained again why this analysis is correct even if factor prices fail to fall. Most people think of an excise tax as raising the price of the taxed product, leaving all other prices, wage rates, and so on, unchanged. This outcome is possible if the monetary authorities permit the price level to rise. Recall, however, that if the price of one good rises and other prices remain unchanged, the overall price level has risen. Labor and capital incomes that remain unchanged in money terms will purchase less than before. Therefore, real labor and capital incomes have fallen. These incomes expressed in dollars of constant purchasing power are now lower, resulting in a burden on the sources side. There is no further net burden on the uses side. In particular, recipients of government transfers bear no burden in this case because their transfers will be increased when the price level rises.

Individual Income Taxes. Taxpayers probably believe that the actual tax payments they make under the federal and state individual income taxes measure their real tax burden. Most economists seem to agree with this judgment. It is important to understand, however, the conditions under which this conclusion is correct. Just as with sales and excise taxes, the economic agents who make the tax payments to the government may not bear the full burden; the tax may be "shifted."

Individual income taxes are basically levies on labor and capital income received by persons (although there are many special provisions that make taxes somewhat less than general taxes on factor incomes). The key question is whether the amounts of labor and saving are affected by the tax. If the quantities supplied are unaffected, the productivities of the factors and their rates of pay will remain unchanged. Under these conditions, the gross (before-tax) incomes of taxpayers are not affected by the tax, and after payment

---

[15] This assumes that the proportions in which factors of production are used in the taxed industry are the same as for all other industries on average. If this is not so, the prices of factors used more intensively in the taxed industry will fall by more than the prices of other factors.

of the tax liabilities their net incomes are lower by exactly the size of the tax. Consequently, taxpayers bear a burden equal to the amount of taxes paid.

Under the assumption that the quantities of labor and saving supplied are unaffected by any tax, the burden of individual income taxes falls on the taxpayers themselves. Although this assumption is certainly open to debate, especially with regard to savings, we will not attempt to weigh the pros and cons here.[16] Most tax experts appear to believe the approach taken here is a good approximation, and the majority of applied tax incidence studies have used this procedure.

If income taxes contained no special treatment of certain types or uses of income, there would be no effects on the relative prices of goods and services. However, certain provisions in the tax law—notably, some of the exclusions and deductions—can be expected to affect relative prices. Whether the effects are substantial is not clear; in any event, there is no net effect on the uses side to be taken into account.

Payroll Taxes. The social security payroll tax is composed of two equal rate levies on covered earnings. In 1976 the first $15,300 of earnings of employees in covered occupations was subject to the tax. Approximately 91 percent of all occupations are subject to the tax; the major exceptions are federal employees and some state and local government employees. Both the employee and the employer paid a tax of 5.85 percent of covered earnings in 1976.

Under competitive conditions, the division of the tax into employer and employee portions has no bearing on its incidence. If employers would pay a wage rate of $2.00 per hour in the absence of the tax but are required to pay the government the employer portion of the social security tax amounting to $0.10 per hour, then they will reduce the wage rate paid to workers to $1.90. Both the employer and employee portions of the tax act to reduce the net earnings of workers for any given volume of employment. This

---

[16] Recent research by Michael J. Boskin has suggested that saving will fall in response to a tax-induced reduction in the interest rate. See "Taxation, Saving, and the Rate of Interest," *Journal of Political Economy*, vol. 86 (April 1978), pp. S3–S52. For a survey of earlier evidence, see Break, "The Incidence and Economic Effects of Taxation." Martin S. Feldstein has examined the implications of variable factor supplies for tax incidence in "Tax Incidence in a Growing Economy with Variable Factor Supply," *Quarterly Journal of Economics*, vol. 88 (November 1975), pp. 551-573, and "Incidence of a Capital Income Tax in a Growing Economy with Variable Savings Rates," *Review of Economic Studies*, vol. 41 (October 1974), pp. 505-513.

argument is not identical to the contention that workers bear the full burden of the tax in proportion to covered earnings. To argue that workers bear the full burden of the social security tax one must also assume that the total amount of labor supplied remains unchanged with the imposition of the tax. If the quantity of labor supplied falls, the before-tax wage rate would rise, and the tax would to some degree be shifted. Under the assumption of an unchanged labor supply, however, the entire burden is borne by workers.[17]

The basis for assuming that labor supply will be unaffected by the social security tax may be somewhat stronger than for other taxes on labor income. In the case of social security, the taxes paid are related, although somewhat loosely, to future pension benefits. For this reason, workers may view the tax simply as forced saving with lower current wages compensated by greater retirement benefits in the future. If the tax is interpreted in this way, workers will not feel that their real wage rates have fallen because of the tax and therefore have no reason to reduce the amount of labor supplied.

Workers might also shift employment to uncovered occupations to avoid the tax. If, however, workers view the tax as a form of forced saving, they would have no reason to do this; they would avoid paying the tax, but they would also lose their future social security pension, so there would be no obvious net gain.

If no net change in the total quantity of labor supplied and no change in the allocation between covered and uncovered jobs occur, the social security tax will have no effect on the prices of goods and services. Consequently, the entire burden of this tax can be allocated to workers in proportion to their covered earnings. A similar analysis applies for the unemployment insurance tax.

Corporation Income Taxes. Corporation income taxes are imposed by the federal government and many state governments. These taxes are levied on the net income (as defined in the tax laws) of incorporated businesses. The tax base is not solely profits, at least as economists define the term. Instead, corporate net income subject to the tax is the return to those who invest in (supply capital to) corporations. Since investors must be induced to provide capital through payment of a reasonable return (just as workers must be induced to work by payment of wages), corporate net income can be viewed as the payment made to a factor of production.

---

[17] A discussion of the theory and evidence relating to the social security payroll tax is given in John A. Brittain, *The Payroll Tax for Social Security* (Washington, D.C.: Brookings Institution, 1972).

Only the return to capital invested in the corporate sector is subject to corporation income taxes. Capital is also employed in the noncorporate sector of the economy (primarily in agriculture and home ownership) where it is not taxed. A factor of production which is taxed in one sector and not in another is subject to the basic market pressure to equalize the net return to that factor in alternative uses. For example, suppose the net rate of return to capital invested in the corporate sector is 4 percent while it is 8 percent in the noncorporate sector. Investors have an incentive to increase their investments in the noncorporate sector where the return is higher and reduce their investment in the corporate sector. Increasing the supply of capital to the noncorporate sector pushes down the rate of return there while reducing the supply of capital to the corporate sector increases the rate of return in that sector. This process will continue until the net rates of return are equal in the two sectors; only then will investors be in equilibrium.

To illustrate how this process determines the incidence of corporate income taxes, assume that the net return to capital in both sectors is 8 percent in the absence of the tax. Next suppose a tax of 50 percent is applied to corporate net income. The short-run effect, before investors have time to change their investments, is to reduce the net return in the corporate sector to 4 percent. Since the yield is still 8 percent in the noncorporate sector, there is incentive for capital to be diverted to that sector where the return is now higher. As a result, the before-tax return rises in the corporate sector and falls in the noncorporate sector. The final equilibrium is reached when the net return is the same in both sectors at, say, 6 percent.

Thus the rate of return received by investors in both sectors of the economy has been reduced from 8 percent to 6 percent by the corporation income tax. All persons receiving income from capital bear a burden from the corporation income tax even though they have not invested in corporations. Under plausible conditions the entire burden of the corporation income tax falls in proportion to capital income regardless of the sector in which the income is generated.[18] Thus, persons who invest in homes or saving accounts bear a burden from the corporation income tax. On the sources of income side of budgets, this study allocates the burden of the tax in proportion to the amount of capital income received.

---

[18] See Arnold C. Harberger, "The Incidence of the Corporation Income Tax," *Journal of Political Economy*, vol. 70 (June 1962), pp. 215-240.

Imposition of a corporation income tax also has effects on the uses side of household budgets. Because corporate investments must yield a higher before-tax return (12 percent in the preceding example), the costs of producing goods in the corporate sector rise. Prices of corporate sector products will increase, and prices in the noncorporate sector will fall. In addition, the net interest rate received by savers will fall, harming savers relative to consumers. For reasons discussed earlier, these individual effects will be ignored, however, on the ground that there will be no net effect on the uses side for any income class.

Property Taxes. Property taxation is employed primarily by local governments. Although there is wide variation in rates and in the definition of taxable property, generally the tax is levied on the assessed value of real property, including land, homes, buildings, and equipment owned by businesses. Property, of course, is simply another name for what economists usually term capital. Taxing the value of property has the same effect as taxing income generated by that property. Consider a business property having a market value of $10,000 and yielding a net income of $800 a year, a return of 8 percent. A property tax of 2 percent of market value, yielding $200 per year, is equivalent to a 25 percent tax on the annual capital income of $800.

If property taxes in all localities were levied at the same rate and on the same base, the question of who bears the tax burden would be straightforward. Since all property would be taxed at the same rate, there would be no incentive for investors to shift capital from one sector of the economy to another. Moreover, under the assumption that the supply of saving is unaffected by any tax, there would be no change in the capital stock and no change in its productivity. Consequently, the before-tax return on investment would be unaffected by the tax, but after-tax capital incomes would fall by the amount of the tax. Owners of capital would bear the entire burden.

With tax rates varying among localities, however, the analysis is slightly different. Investors, concerned with the net of tax return, have incentive to reduce investment (holdings of capital) in communities with higher than average tax rates and increase investments in communities with lower than average tax rates. Analysis of the burden of the property tax is performed in a way analogous to that of the corporation income tax. Since the net return to capital in all localities will tend to be equalized, a burden will be borne by all owners of property, even those in localities that do not impose a property tax. The magnitude of the burden on owners of capital depends on the national average rate of tax on property. Thus, on the sources of income side of budgets, local property taxes can be allocated in proportion to capital income in the same way as the burden of a national property tax would be treated.[19]

There are differential effects from a system of local property taxes on the uses side. Before-tax rates of return must be higher in communities with higher than average tax rates. The prices of goods produced with capital in these communities will be higher because of the tax while prices of goods produced in communities with lower than average tax rates will fall with the imposition of the tax. These effects are quite relevant when the concern is with the effect of a local property tax on residents of a given community. Insofar as the concern of this study is nationwide, these effects on relative prices can be assumed to cancel out.[20] Consumers of goods produced in heavily taxed localities lose, but consumers of goods produced in lightly taxed localities gain.

Alternative Incidence Assumptions. The preceding analysis has explained how the burdens of the major taxes should be allocated if the U.S. economy adjusts to the taxes in the same manner as a perfectly competitive economy. Primarily because the U.S. economy is not perfectly competitive, a number of economists remain skeptical of the results generated. Most of the controversy has centered on two taxes: the corporation income tax and property taxes. To a lesser extent, some economists have been uneasy with the conclusion that the employer portion of the social security tax is borne by workers.

Even though the economy is not perfectly competitive, it does not necessarily follow that the results of an analysis based on competitive assumptions will be wrong. Indeed, at least three studies have shown the competitive results to apply even under certain specified noncompetitive conditions. Arnold C. Harberger, in his analysis of the corporation income tax, showed that even if all corporations were monopolies engaging in mark-up pricing, the

---

[19] For further discussion of the complex issues involved here, see Peter M. Mieszkowski, "The Property Tax: An Excise or a Profits Tax?" *Journal of Public Economics*, vol. 1 (April 1972), pp. 73-96; and Aaron, *Who Pays the Property Tax?*

[20] Charles E. McLure, Jr., emphasizes that the appropriate analysis depends on whether the emphasis is on effects within a locality or nationwide, in "The 'New View' of the Property Tax: A Caveat," *National Tax Journal*, vol. 30 (March 1977), pp. 59-68.

results would be virtually the same as in the competitive case.[21] Basing his remarks on the Harberger study, Aaron has argued that the analysis of the property tax under competitive assumptions yields the correct conclusion even in the absence of competition.[22] Finally, John A. Brittain has explained why the employer portion of the social security payroll tax will be borne by workers even in many instances in which employers do not operate in perfectly competitive markets.[23]

These studies do not imply that the competitive results are correct for any type of noncompetitive behavior; they only conclude that these results hold for certain specified departures from the competitive assumptions. There is, however, the clear implication that the results based on a competitive model may be correct for a wide variety of noncompetitive cases as well. As yet, there has been little rigorous theoretical analysis of tax incidence in a noncompetitive setting to serve as a basis for applied tax incidence studies.

Nonetheless, many tax experts are too uncomfortable with the competitive results to rely on them exclusively. To take this problem into account, the procedure usually followed in tax incidence studies is to substitute alternative assumptions in the analysis of the incidence of the more controversial taxes. These alternative assumptions are not based on any definite theory but simply represent conceivable ways in which the economy might respond to taxes. As such, they represent a way of determining the range of possible outcomes.

The most common alternative incidence assumption for the three controversial taxes is to assume that some arbitrary part of each tax is shifted to consumers. Corporations, for example, are assumed to respond, at least in part, to the corporate income tax as if it were an excise tax placed on their products. In accord with this assumption, some portion of the tax is allocated in the same way as an excise tax.

We follow this procedure by making an alternative calculation of the distribution of tax burdens based on the assumption that half of the corporation income tax, half of the property tax, and half of the employer portion of the payroll tax have the same effects as excise or sales taxes. It should be recalled, however, that in contrast to previous studies using similar assumptions, these taxes are not allocated in proportion to consumption outlays. As explained in detail earlier, excise and sales taxes should be allocated in proportion

---

[21] See Harberger, "Incidence of the Corporation Income Tax."

[22] See Aaron, *Who Pays the Property Tax?*

[23] See Brittain, *The Payroll Tax for Social Security.*

TABLE 2

Comparison of Incidence Assumptions
Used to Calculate the Distribution of Tax Burdens

Tax	Competitive Assumptions	Alternative Assumptions
Sales and excise	Factor income	Factor income
Individual income tax	Tax payments	Tax payments
Payroll taxes		
Employer	Covered earnings	Half to factor income; half to covered earnings
Employee	Covered earnings	Covered earnings
Corporation income tax	Capital income	Half to factor income; half to capital income
Property tax	Capital income	Half to factor income; half to capital income

to factor income, not in proportion to consumption. Consequently, if some part of, say, the corporation income tax is shifted to consumers in the same manner as an excise or sales tax, that part of the tax must instead be allocated in proportion to factor income.

Table 2 presents a summary of the alternative sets of incidence assumptions that will be used to calculate the distribution of tax burdens by income class.

A Methodological Issue

The major difference between this and previous tax incidence studies is in the allocation of tax burdens under sales and excise taxes. We assign these taxes in proportion to factor income while previous studies allocate them in proportion to consumption. This difference in analysis has important implications for the estimated tax burdens of various income classes. When allocated according to factor income, sales and excise taxes are progressive elements in the tax system, but when allocated according to consumption, they are very regressive elements. This difference in analysis becomes even more important if noncompetitive incidence assumptions are judged appropriate for other taxes in the system since these assumptions are tantamount to assuming that the economy responds to other taxes as if they were sales or excise taxes.

Earlier in this chapter, we defended our approach in part by pointing out that most government transfers are linked to the prices of particular goods or to the price level, or both. This practical defense may not be fully convincing because not all transfers are explicitly related to consumer prices. In addition, the levels of transfer payments that are linked in this way could be changed by deliberate legislative action. These problems point out the difficulty of determining how sales and excise taxes affect both the price level and money value of transfers. Insofar as sales and excise taxes affect these two variables, it is clear that hundreds of other factors also affect the price level and money transfer payments. To disentangle the independent influence of sales and excise (or other) taxes would be difficult to do with any precision.

Consequently, we believe it may be useful to consider this issue from a methodological perspective, emphasizing the logic and internal consistency of the framework underlying tax incidence analysis. Under the balanced-budget approach, when the incidence of any tax is analyzed, some assumptions must be made about other taxes and government expenditures. The assumption that underlies our analysis is simply that other taxes and government expenditures remain unchanged in real terms. Note that this assumption implies that transfers are constant in real terms since transfers constitute part of the general category of government expenditures. Thus, our assumption of fixed real transfers is really part of a general assumption intended to keep the real effects of other government policies constant so as to isolate the effects of the tax in question. This basic assumption is maintained through the analysis of each separate tax.

To understand the significance of the assumption of fixed real transfers, consider the alternative assumption that the real value of transfers falls in proportion to the tax as a percentage of national income, which would justify allocating sales and excise taxes in proportion to consumption. An excise tax that produces revenue equal to 2 percent of national income is assumed to be accompanied by a 2 percent reduction in the real value of all transfers. The transfers will then purchase 2 percent less than before the tax. This fall in the real value of transfers would occur if the price level rose by 2 percent and the money value of transfers were unchanged or if the price level remained unchanged and the money value of transfers were reduced 2 percent (among other ways).

There are several problems with making this assumption in tax incidence analysis. First, it is arbitrary to assume that one type of government expenditures, transfer payments, falls in real terms while other types of government expenditures (presumably) do not. Why should government transfers which accrue largely to low-income households be singled out as the only type of government expenditure to fall? Moreover, if the real value of transfers declines, then the real value of taxes to finance these transfers must also be reduced. Thus, it is necessary to assume that the real burden of some other taxes is reduced at the same time that real transfers fall. The analysis is incomplete unless a reduction in other taxes is incorporated, but clearly this expansion of the analysis requires a further arbitrary assumption as to which tax or taxes are to perform this role.

Another problem becomes apparent in the analysis of taxes other than sales and excise taxes. Consider the corporation income tax, on the assumption that competitive incidence assumptions are appropriate. Must the real value of transfers also be assumed to fall in proportion to this tax? Clearly, even under competitive conditions the overall price level may rise just as much because of the corporation income tax as because of an excise tax. Yet previous tax incidence studies have held that the corporation income tax falls on owners of capital under competitive conditions regardless whether the overall price level is affected. This is correct only if real transfers are assumed to be unaffected. Thus, it appears that previous studies have inadvertently relied on different and inconsistent assumptions in the analysis of the corporation income tax and excise taxes. In the case of excise taxes, real transfers are assumed to fall, while in the case of corporate taxes they are assumed to remain unchanged. This same issue also arises with respect to all other taxes. The results of other studies depend on the assumption that real transfers fall under sales and excise taxes, but not under any other taxes, implying an unintended internal inconsistency in the theoretical framework used to analyze different taxes.

There has also been an inconsistency in the framework used to analyze the same tax under competitive and noncompetitive assumptions. As has been demonstrated, to hold that the corporation income tax falls on owners of capital under competitive conditions requires the assumption that real transfers are unaffected. Under noncompetitive conditions, however, if part of the tax is judged to be borne in proportion to consumption, it is necessary to assume that real transfers fall. There seems no reason to believe that the effects of the corporation income tax on the level of real transfers should depend on the degree of competition in the corporate sector of the economy.

This unintentional inconsistency in tax studies has probably occurred because of the type of rigorous theoretical analysis that has been developed in the economics literature. The formal theoretical models of tax incidence assume an economy in which the incomes of households are solely in the form of labor and capital income; there is no transfer income. The conclusions of these analyses have then been utilized in applied tax incidence studies without recognizing the modifications required when government transfers are an important source of income.

While these remarks do not purport to demonstrate that the approach adopted in this study is necessarily the only plausible one, we have tried to point out the difficulties and inconsistencies that underlie previous studies. Our assumption that any given tax leaves the real magnitudes of other taxes and expenditures unchanged does provide a logical and internally consistent basis for tax incidence analysis. In addition, it is a plausible approach given the way in which most transfers are linked to prices, and it has the advantage of implying that the distribution of tax burdens is independent of the effect of taxes on absolute prices. Nonetheless, further study of the methodological foundations of tax incidence theory incorporating the importance of government transfers is clearly needed.

3

Data Sources and Methodology

In this chapter, the techniques used to arrive at the estimates of tax burdens are explained in detail. We first describe our data sources and the imputations and assumptions made in estimating the amount of income received and taxes paid by each household. The second half of the chapter describes some aggregate characteristics of the household sample with respect to income and taxes paid and the composition of the sources of income.

Data Sources, Imputations, and Assumptions

In applying the theoretical analysis of Chapter 2 to estimate the burden of taxes across households in the United States, it is impossible simply to turn to readily available statistics. Instead, we were forced to piece together data from various sources and to make imputations and assumptions in many cases in order to draw a complete picture of the income and tax status of U.S. households. The starting point for the estimates was the Current Population Survey (CPS) for March 1975, conducted by the U.S. Census Bureau, which collected 1974 income and demographic data for a representative sample of 47,414 U.S. households. The data were subsequently updated to correspond to 1976 levels.[1] This representative sample, projected by the appropriate weights, can be considered an accurate picture of the entire U.S. population in 1976.

Unfortunately, the CPS data do not contain many components of household income that economists generally agree should be in-

---

[1] See U.S. Congress, Congressional Budget Office, "Poverty Status of Families under Alternative Definitions of Income," Background Paper no. 17, January 1977, p. 19.

cluded. Furthermore, many taxes paid by households, both directly and indirectly, are not recorded in the survey. Therefore the two major types of imputations necessary concerned sources of income and taxes paid.

Income. In measuring household income, we have adopted the so-called Haig-Simons definition of income to the extent possible, given data limitations and other considerations. The Haig-Simons definition states that a household's income consists of the amount of consumption that a household enjoys in a given period plus any change in the household's net worth. We have chosen to ignore the value of leisure time as part of consumption although certainly leisure is included in the income, or well-being, of the household. We also exclude the benefits families receive from general government expenditures such as schools or highways. However, even limiting consumption in the Haig-Simons income measure to private goods and services, several items which constitute important parts of many households' income were not recorded by the Current Population Survey. These omissions were: some cash transfer payments, in-kind transfer payments, imputed rent from owner-occupied housing, and accrued capital gains.

The first two items, cash and in-kind transfers, are important sources of income to the households at the lower end of the income distribution. For that reason, and because the tax incidence assumptions advanced in this study allocate indirect taxes in proportion to factor income, it was essential to include the transfer income received by each household. Fortunately, transfer income had already been imputed to the households in the CPS sample.[2] Although complicated, the imputation procedure was essentially based on a comparison of each household's income and demographic characteristics with the requirements of various government transfer programs. Fortunately, the transfer income imputation procedure took into account the fact that fewer households participate in many transfer programs than were apparently legally entitled to do so. Thus, in the transfer income imputation process, total imputed transfer benefits for the sample were consistent with national aggregate expenditures on each program.

Among the cash transfer programs included in the imputation were Aid to Families with Dependent Children (AFDC), Supplemen-

---

[2] The imputation was performed by Mathematica Policy Research for the Congressional Budget Office. We are very grateful to John Korbel of CBO for making the data available to us.

tal Security Income (SSI), unemployment insurance, social security, and veterans' pensions and disability payments. The in-kind transfer programs included the cash value of food stamps, public housing and rent subsidy programs, and federal child nutrition programs. In addition, the value of medical assistance programs (Medicare and Medicaid) was imputed.[3]

The two other types of income that were not recorded by the CPS were the imputed net rental value of owner-occupied housing and accrued capital gains on stock owned by households. According to the Haig-Simons income definition, the use of owner-occupied housing constitutes consumption even though the owner pays no rent in order to live in his own house. This nonmarket transaction clearly represents consumption by the household and should be included as income. Similarly, accrued capital gains on corporate stock represent income; although the change in value of stock holdings may not be realized by the household during the year, the household will experience a change in the value of assets, or ability to consume, which should be included as income.[4]

Imputed rent was allocated to the households in the CPS file on the basis of unpublished distributions of this item by household income prepared from the Brookings Institution's MERGE file.[5] Since the Brookings distribution referred to 1973 rather than 1976, we made the simplifying assumption that the dollar relationship between income and imputed rent was the same in 1973 and 1976. Thus, if the average household with $10,000 income in 1973 had $250 in imputed rent in 1973, we assumed that the same proportional relationship could be applied in 1976.

Capital gains on corporate stock were imputed by assuming that in the long run capital gains equaled retained earnings of corporations. The ratio of total retained earnings to total dividends for the 1974–1977 period was multiplied by the amount of stock dividends each household received during the year. The longer-term average

---

[3] The treatment of medical programs is perhaps not the best that might be devised. Instead of measuring the insurance value of Medicaid and Medicare (that is, the value of private health insurance that would provide the same coverage), the imputation procedure apparently was based on actual medical expenses. Thus, a household covered by Medicare or Medicaid but needing no medical services during the year would be recorded as receiving no benefit, while the person covered by medical programs who happened to need a great deal of medical care during the year is recorded as receiving a large benefit. This procedure somewhat artificially makes the benefits appear unequally distributed among all Medicare and Medicaid participants.

[4] We defer the question of inflation-induced changes in asset values. For the time being, nominal changes in asset values will be treated as real changes.

[5] We thank Joseph Minarik of Brookings for making these data available to us.

ratio of retained earnings to dividends was employed to avoid any short-run fluctuations of the ratio over the business cycle.

Two other important assumptions were made about household income. All sources of income had to be classified as labor income, capital income, or transfer income. For most types of income the proper classification is obvious: wages and salaries are labor income, while dividends, interest, and capital gains are capital income. For some types of income, however, the correct classification is not unequivocally clear. For example, despite the contributory aspect of the social security program, we chose to treat social security income as transfer income because benefits are financed out of current taxes even though each person's benefit does bear a tenuous relationship to the taxes he previously paid. Following this line of reasoning, social security taxes were considered to be taxes on labor rather than forced saving.

A more delicate question arises with respect to income from public and private pension programs. Consider first government pensions such as those for veterans and government employees. Since these pensions are largely unfunded and depend on tax revenue (as opposed to income from capital), they were again treated as transfer payments. One reason for this decision was the fact that taxes on capital income would not diminish the amount of funds available for public pensions as they would private pensions.

The receipt of income from private pension plans poses a problem for any analysis of tax burdens. Strictly speaking, according to the Haig-Simons income definition, contributions to pension funds (whether by employee or employer) should be counted as labor income when they are made, requiring an imputation to household income of the employer's contribution to pension funds. The interest earned from such pension fund accumulations should be counted as capital income in the year it is earned (not disbursed). Furthermore, viewed in this way, the actual receipt of benefits from private pension funds constitutes dissaving or drawing down existing assets rather than income in the Haig-Simons sense.

Instead of treating pension benefits in this way (which would probably be most theoretically pleasing to economists), private pension receipts have been counted as capital income in the year they are received, rather than in the year earned. A few reasons for this treatment of pension income are outlined below:

1. The data on employer contributions to pension funds are very sketchy and no data are available on the interest currently being earned on pension fund accumulations by individual households.

2. Since pensions are a major mechanism for transferring resources of the household over the life cycle, attributing pension income in the Haig-Simons way exaggerates the inequality of annual incomes relative to permanent incomes. Imputing the tax burden of capital taxes (on pension fund assets) to the relatively high incomes of individuals currently working would create an upward bias in our estimate of the progressivity of the tax system. Our method, which counts pension receipts as income in the generally lower-income retirement years, allocates the tax burden of capital taxes to these lower-income households. This method biases the results in the direction of finding the tax system to be less progressive than it would appear on the basis of lifetime incomes. Put differently, households are generally accumulating pension assets during the high-income parts of their life cycle and drawing down these assets at the low-income retirement end of the life cycle; their lifetime income (or permanent income) is somewhere between these extremes. Attributing taxes on pension earnings to the high-income years will make the tax system appear more progressive than it really is (on a lifetime income basis) while our method probably errs in the opposite direction in making the tax burden on low-income, retired households appear heavier than it actually is.

3. Counting the pension disbursement as capital income recognizes the fact that most of the accumulated pension assets at the time of retirement consist of interest income rather than dissaving. If the average pension dollar has been saved for twenty years at 8 percent interest, seventy-five cents of each pension dollar come from interest earnings.

Taxes. Although the CPS file records state and federal income taxes paid as well as the employee portion of the social security tax, all other taxes borne by the household had to be apportioned indirectly. Methods of apportionment are described for the four major groups of taxes: income taxes, payroll taxes, property and corporation income taxes, and excise and sales taxes. Estate and gift taxes were not included in this analysis.

Income taxes. Since state and federal income taxes were recorded directly by the CPS for each household, no imputations were necessary.

Payroll taxes. The employee's share of the social security tax was already recorded in the data file. Under assumptions of competition and fixed supplies of productive factors, the employer's share of the tax is also borne by the worker in the form of lower earnings. Hence the worker's pretax earnings will be higher than his recorded earnings by the amount of the employer's share of payroll taxes. For the social security tax, the employer's share is exactly equal to the employee's payment recorded by the Census Bureau.

The other major payroll tax is the unemployment insurance (UI) tax, which was not recorded on the household data file, since it is nominally paid by employers. Unfortunately, the unemployment insurance tax system is so complicated and varies so much from state to state that precise imputation is impossible. We approximated UI taxes by assuming a 2 percent rate of each worker's earned income up to $4,000. This simplification corresponds fairly well to the average tax rates and taxable earnings ceilings across states.[6]

Taxes on capital income. There are two major types of indirect taxes on the income from capital in the U.S. tax system—corporation income taxes and property taxes. Although neither tax is levied directly on all types of capital income, under the assumptions explained previously, the net of tax rate of return on all types of capital will be equalized by the flows of capital from one use to another. It follows from these assumptions that all capital income is reduced equally by the amount of taxes on capital income. Aggregate taxes on capital (property taxes and state and federal corporate income taxes) were $124.3 billion dollars in 1976,[7] and net capital income, including imputed rent, capital gains, proprietor's income attributable to capital, dividends, and interest was $178.2 billion. Thus the rate of capital taxation on net capital income was 0.69 (124.3/178.2). This means that for each dollar a household received in net capital income, its pretax capital income was $1.69 and the capital taxes paid were $0.69.

Sales and excise taxes. As discussed in Chapter 2, the burden of sales and excise taxes is assumed to fall evenly on all factor income. That is, factor income is assumed to be reduced by the gross amount of sales and excise taxes. In 1976, aggregate federal indirect business taxes and state and local sales and gross receipts taxes were $77.9 billion.[8] Since aggregate factor income (gross of income, capital, and

---

[6] See Tax Foundation, Inc., *Facts and Figures on Government Finance 1977* (New York, 1977), pp. 218-219.

[7] See *Economic Report of the President, 1978*, pp. 343-345. This breaks down into $55.9 billion in federal corporate income taxes, $59.5 billion in state and local property taxes, and $8.9 billion in state and local corporate income taxes.

[8] *Economic Report of the President, 1978*, p. 345. We have not included any nontax payments, which include license fees, profits of state alcohol monopolies, and the like.

payroll taxes) was $1,296.2 billion, the average indirect tax rate on factor income is 0.06. Hence to compute each household's income in the absence of indirect taxes, we simply multiplied the household's factor income by 1.06.

A Brief Example. It may be instructive at this point to consider a brief example to illustrate our calculations. Consider a representative household with $15,000 of wage income and $1,000 of interest income as reported by the CPS and income taxes and social security taxes of $1,300 and $600 respectively. As Table 3 shows, to determine labor income we first added the amounts of payroll tax paid by the employer. In this case, the $600 matching share of social security taxes and $80 of unemployment insurance taxes were added. Capital income must be augmented by the imputation of net rent on owner-occupied housing ($264) and then increased by the household's proportionate share of capital taxes. Since 0.69 of $1,264 is $872, capital income gross of capital taxes was $2,136. Note that if the household had received dividends, the dividends would have been used to impute capital gains on corporate stock.

Factor income gross of all taxes except indirect taxes is $17,816 ($15,680 + $2,136). The final step in arriving at before-tax income is to impute the burden of indirect taxes, which, as discussed above, fall at the rate of 0.06 on factor income. In this case, indirect taxes would come to $1,067, giving the household a before-tax, before-transfer (BTBT) income of $18,883, which represents what the household would have received in the absence of any tax or transfer programs.

The income base upon which the household's taxes are levied includes both factor income and transfer income. Suppose that transfer income for this representative household had been imputed to be $650 in cash transfers and $125 in in-kind transfers. Adding the total transfers of $775 to BTBT income yields $19,658 of before-tax, after-transfer (BTAT) income. This figure will be used as the base for calculating average rates of taxation since it represents the household's income in the absence of the tax system.

The final step in computing the tax burden is merely to sum all the taxes paid by the household. In this example, total taxes were $4,519. It is important to remember that the tax burden of the household includes not only the taxes actually remitted by the household but also the taxes which reduce its income in less direct ways, such as payroll and corporation income taxes. For our representative household more than half the tax burden is not physically remitted

TABLE 3
INCOME AND TAXES OF A REPRESENTATIVE HOUSEHOLD

Item	Amount (dollars)	Source
Labor income		
Gross wages	15,000	CPS
Employer share of social security tax	600	Equal to employee share of CPS
Unemployment insurance tax	80	0.02 × $4,000 earnings ceiling
Subtotal	15,680	
Capital income		
Interest	1,000	CPS
Imputed rent	264	Brookings data
Capital tax	872	0.69 × capital income
Subtotal	2,136	
Factor income net of sales and excise taxes	17,816	
Sales and excise taxes	1,067	0.06 × factor income
Before-tax, before-transfer income	18,883	
Transfers		
Cash	650	Imputed by
In-kind	125	Mathematica
Subtotal	775	Policy Research
Before-tax, after-transfer income	19,658	
Taxes		
Sales and excise	1,067	Imputed
Payroll	1,280	CPS and imputed
Income	1,300	CPS
On capital income	872	Imputed
Subtotal	4,519	
After-tax, after-transfer income	15,139	
Average tax rate = 4,519/19,658 = 23.0%		

by the household. The after-tax, after-transfer (ATAT) income of the household is $15,139, and the average tax rate on the household was 23.0 percent (4,519/$19,658). That is, the household's income was reduced by over one-fifth by the tax system.

Characteristics of the Sample

Before turning to the calculated distribution of the tax burden in Chapter 4, consider a few of the characteristics of total households in the United States as projected from the sample used in this study. Table 4 displays the aggregate figures for the population of households. In 1976 total BTBT income was $1,374.1 billion, of which 77 percent was labor income and 23 percent capital income. Total cash and in-kind transfers were $200.2 billion, while aggregate taxes were $458.6 billion, leaving an aggregate disposable income after taxes and transfers (ATAT) of $1,115.7 billion. Before-tax, after-transfer (BTAT) income totaled $1,574.3 billion, and the aggregate tax rate was about 29 percent (458.6/1,574.3).

Of course, these aggregate figures obscure some interesting and important differences between households at different income levels with respect to sources of income. These differences are important from the point of view of tax incidence analysis for two reasons: First, capital income tends to be taxed at higher rates than labor income so that the composition of factor income affects a household's tax burden apart from the size of its income; second, according to the incidence assumptions in this study, the burden of indirect taxes falls on factor income so that differences in income shares derived from factor earnings (as opposed to transfer income) will affect a household's tax burden. The figures in Table 5 are relevant to both of these points.

TABLE 4
AGGREGATE INCOME AND TAXES, 1976
(billions of dollars)

Item		Amount
Before-tax, before-transfer income		1,374.1
Less taxes		458.6
Sales and excise	77.9	
Payroll	98.3	
Income	158.1	
Property and corporation	124.3	
Total taxes	458.6	
Net factor income		915.5
Plus transfers		200.2
After-tax, after-transfer income		1,115.7
Plus taxes		458.6
Before-tax, after-transfer income		1,574.3

TABLE 5

Source of Income by Deciles of
Before-Tax, After-Transfer (BTAT) Income

	Percentage of Decile BTAT Income			
Decile	Labor	Capital	Cash transfers	In-kind transfers
1	26.0	14.3	47.2	12.5
2	34.3	10.9	36.9	17.9
3	48.0	11.6	28.2	12.3
4	61.0	11.5	20.7	6.8
5	70.9	10.7	14.6	3.8
6	77.2	10.2	10.5	2.1
7	80.7	9.9	8.1	1.3
8	81.5	10.6	7.0	0.9
9	79.8	13.7	5.8	0.7
10	55.7	40.0	3.9	0.4

In Table 5 households are arranged by deciles of BTAT income, and the share of total income for each decile is given for each type of income. Thus, for example, households in the fifth decile derived 70.9 percent of total income from labor earnings. Table 5 is striking in two respects. The first is the large degree to which households in the lowest two income deciles depend on transfer income. Transfers constitute over half the income of these households. Neither are transfers insignificant for higher income families because some of these households receive social security, Medicare, and unemployment insurance. Second, capital income constitutes a rather small share of income for all households except those in the top decile. We found this degree of inequality of capital income somewhat surprising and suspect it would be less extreme if the earnings from pension fund assets were included as capital income for those currently working.[9] In any case, these facts relating to the sources of income for U.S. households mean that the burden of indirect taxes will be relatively light for those in the bottom deciles (since that burden falls on factor income, which constitutes a relatively small share of total income) and that the tax rate on the highest decile is likely to be high because capital income is taxed more heavily than labor income. In the next chapter we examine these tax burdens in detail.

---

[9] We suspect that small amounts of capital income may be underreported for many households.

4

Tax Burdens and Tax Rates

Table 6 summarizes the central findings of this study. To derive these results, we ranked households from lowest to highest by household BTAT income and then divided the population of households into deciles. For each decile the average rate of tax was then computed for the four basic groups of taxes in the U.S. tax system: sales and excise taxes, payroll taxes, income taxes, and property and corporation income taxes. These last two taxes are given together because, in our analysis, both are allocated in proportion to capital income. The tax rates are calculated by estimating the total tax burden of all households in each decile and dividing by the total BTAT income of that decile. The estimated tax rates, therefore, do not apply to every household but instead represent an average of all households in each decile. Table 6 also indicates the tax rates for the top 1 percent of all households as well as the average for the population as a whole.

Competitive Incidence Assumptions

The most important conclusion to be drawn from Table 6 is that the overall effect of the U.S. tax system is quite progressive; the average rate of tax rises continually and substantially from 11.7 percent to 38.3 percent from the lowest income decile to the highest. Some feeling for the degree of progressivity of the tax system can be obtained by noting that the combined tax rate for the top decile is over three times the rate for the bottom decile. Tax rates for the entire tax system rise sharply from the first to the fifth decile of households, then increase somewhat less steeply from the fifth to the ninth decile, and again rise sharply for the top tenth of the population. The upper 1 percent of households faces a combined tax rate of nearly 50 percent.

TABLE 6

AVERAGE TAX RATES BY INCOME DECILE

(percent)

	Type of Tax				
Income Decile	Sales and excise	Payroll	Income	Property and corporation income	Combined
1	2.3	3.3	0.7	5.5	11.7
2	2.6	3.9	1.8	4.2	12.5
3	3.4	5.4	3.0	4.5	16.3
4	4.1	6.9	4.7	4.4	20.2
5	4.7	8.0	6.4	4.1	23.2
6	5.0	8.5	8.1	3.9	25.5
7	5.2	8.2	9.5	3.8	26.7
8	5.3	7.9	10.8	4.1	28.1
9	5.3	7.2	12.2	5.3	30.0
10	5.5	3.8	13.6	15.4	38.3
Top 1 percent	5.6	1.1	12.4	28.8	47.9
All deciles	4.9	6.2	10.0	7.9	29.1

Of the four major groups of taxes, all place a higher tax rate on the top decile than on the bottom. In particular, the average tax rate imposed by sales and excise taxes rises from 2.3 percent for the lowest decile to 5.5 percent for the top decile because, according to our incidence assumptions, the burden of these indirect taxes falls only on factor income, and the proportion of factor income in total household income rises with the level of household income. In contrast, most previous tax incidence studies have allocated the burden of sales and excise taxes according to consumption expenditures and have thus found these taxes to be regressive because consumption spending is a lower proportion of annual income for higher income households. As explained in Chapter 2, we believe this approach to be incorrect.

Income taxes are the most progressive element of the tax system with the highest ratio of rate paid by the top decile to rate paid by the lowest decile. This progressivity stems from both the inherent progressivity of effective rates in the income tax system and the fact that transfer income, which is not taxed, constitutes a major source of income for the bottom range of the income distribution. Recall that our estimates are based on actual reported taxes paid rather than the statutory tax rate schedule.

The only tax for which rates decline at higher income levels is the payroll tax. Even payroll taxes, however, are progressive up to the sixth decile, becoming regressive above that level. Contrary to the accepted wisdom that payroll taxes are regressive, these taxes do not impose a greater than average burden on the bottom third of the income distribution. The low rates on the low-income households reflect the small share of labor income in their total income, while the regressivity at upper-income levels results from the ceiling on taxable earnings and the exclusion of capital income from payroll taxation.

The outstanding feature of the burden of property and corporation income taxes is the much higher rate of tax on the highest decile than on the lower nine. Since these taxes are assumed to fall equally on all sources of income from capital, the pattern of tax rates in Table 6 parallels the pattern of capital income in Table 5. Our information, however, about capital income is quite poor because of the crudity of the imputed rent procedure, the likely underreporting of dividend receipts, and lack of information on pension assets. Given this margin of error, the pattern of property and corporation income tax rates might best be described as essentially proportional for the first nine deciles (ranging from 3.8 to 5.5 percent) with a substantially higher rate on the top tenth of households generating from the greater proportion of income these households derived from capital. The relatively high rate of these taxes reported for the lowest decile is caused by the large amount of imputed rent (that is, the consumption value of the housing they own) relative to their annual income.

Table 7 presents the same information shown in Table 6 except that households are grouped into dollar income classes rather than income deciles. In interpreting the tax rates applicable to various income levels, the reader must remember that for most households our calculation of pretax (BTAT) income is substantially greater than income as normally perceived by households, both because we have imputed some sources of income not received in monetary form and because we have estimated what income would have been in the absence of taxes. As in Table 6, the tax rates in Table 7 reveal the great disparity among the average tax burdens of households at different income levels.

TABLE 7
Average Tax Rates by Income Class
(percent)

Income (thousands of dollars)	Number of House- holds (millions)	Type of Tax				
		Sales and excise	Payroll	Income	Property and corporation income	Combined
0–5	7.58	2.3	3.3	0.7	5.5	11.7
5–10	14.37	3.0	4.7	2.4	4.4	14.5
10–15	13.65	4.3	7.3	5.3	4.2	21.0
15–20	11.93	5.0	8.4	8.0	4.0	25.3
20–25	9.06	5.2	8.2	9.9	3.9	27.1
25–30	6.59	5.3	7.7	11.2	4.5	28.8
30–40	6.52	5.3	7.1	12.6	5.4	30.4
40–50	2.92	5.4	5.9	13.8	7.8	32.9
50–100	2.76	5.5	3.7	14.4	13.5	37.0
100+	0.69	5.6	1.1	12.4	28.9	48.0

Alternative Incidence Assumptions

In calculating our basic tax incidence results, we have assumed that markets for capital and labor are perfectly competitive. Because many people feel that these markets do not behave competitively, another set of incidence results was constructed based on the non-competitive assumptions described in Table 2. Under these assumptions, half of the employer contribution of the payroll tax and half of taxes on capital income (property and corporation income taxes) are treated as having the same effect as sales and excise taxes in raising the price of goods relative to payments to all factors of production. These noncompetitive assumptions provide an alternative to the competitive assumptions underlying Table 6 in which firms are unable to pass on the tax in higher prices, imposing the burden on the specific productive factors taxed.

The slight differences between the tax rates in Table 6 and those in Table 8 indicate that abandoning the competitive assumptions does not alter our earlier conclusion that the overall tax system is highly progressive. In other words, our results are robust to changes in assumptions about the competitiveness of markets. Previous incidence studies have found that imposing noncompetitive assumptions reduced the progressivity of the overall tax system because other taxes were assumed to act like sales and excise taxes, which were treated as regressive taxes. In contrast, since sales and excise taxes are progressive in our incidence framework, noncompetitive assumptions do not reduce overall tax progressivity. Assuming that parts of payroll taxes and taxes on capital are shifted forward to consumers like an indirect tax does not make them regressive taxes. In fact, note that the payroll tax becomes more progressive under these noncompetitive assumptions because it now reduces the full factor income of upper-income households rather than just labor earnings up to the ceiling on taxable earnings.

A detailed comparison of Tables 6 and 8 reveals that the noncompetitive incidence assumptions result in very slight decreases in the taxes paid by the extremes of the income distribution and small increases in the tax burden on the middle-income deciles. The reduced burden on the lowest-income families can be attributed to the relatively small burden that sales and excise taxes impose on these households, while the reduction of tax burden on the wealthiest families stems from the diminished burden of capital taxation.

We conclude that treating payroll taxes and property and corporation income taxes as if they raised the prices of goods relative to all factor income rather than reducing real labor income or real capital income respectively (as under the competitive incidence assumptions) does not alter the major findings of this study. Our finding of progressivity does not depend on the assumptions of a competitive economy, at least within the range of noncompetitive assumptions usually employed in tax incidence studies. Since the estimates do not vary significantly with incidence assumptions, only the results for the competitive incidence assumptions will be reported in the remainder of this chapter.

Distribution of Pretax and Posttax Incomes

Since average tax rates on households rise steeply with income, it is clear that the overall effect of the tax system alone is to reduce inequality in after-tax incomes. One way of measuring the redistributive effect of the tax system is to compare the before- and after-tax share of total income received by households of a certain rank in the income distribution. The first column of Table 9 shows the distribution of pretax income (BTAT income) across the range of households in the United States, ranked by their before-tax incomes. In a world of perfect income equality, each decile would receive

TABLE 8

Average Tax Rates by Income Decile:
Noncompetitive Incidence Assumptions
(percent)

	Type of Tax				
Income Decile	Sales and excise	Payroll	Income	Property and corporation income	Combined
1	2.2	3.2	0.7	4.5	10.7
2	2.5	3.7	1.8	4.1	12.2
3	3.4	5.1	3.0	4.9	16.4
4	4.1	6.4	4.7	5.5	20.7
5	4.6	7.4	6.3	5.7	24.1
6	5.0	7.8	8.0	5.9	26.6
7	5.1	7.7	9.3	5.9	28.1
8	5.2	7.5	10.6	6.1	29.4
9	5.3	7.0	12.1	6.8	31.2
10	5.4	4.7	14.0	12.2	36.4

exactly the same share of total before-tax income, or 10 percent. Perfect inequality in the extreme would imply that the top decile would receive all (100 percent) of pretax income. Obviously, the actual distribution is somewhere between these extremes with the lowest income decile receiving 1.47 percent of total pretax income and the top decile obtaining about twenty times that amount, or 31.2 percent of total income.

These figures relating to households exaggerate the inequality in the distribution of per capita income because there are on average 1.46 persons per household in the lowest decile while households in the top decile average 3.38 persons. Hence, the disparity in income per person is much less than appears in Table 9. In addition, annual data exaggerate measured income inequality by incorporating temporary deviations from permanent income. For these and other reasons the after-tax income shares should not be interpreted as measures of the degree of economic inequality, but the difference between the before-tax and after-tax shares do suggest the equalizing effect of the tax system.

Comparison of the before- and after-tax distribution of income shows that the tax system has significantly reduced the degree of inequality in the distribution of net income. The share of the bottom

TABLE 9
EFFECT OF TAX SYSTEM ON THE DISTRIBUTION OF INCOME
(percentage shares)

Income Decile	Income Share Before Taxes	Income Share After Taxes
1	1.5	1.8
2	3.2	3.9
3	4.4	5.2
4	5.7	6.4
5	7.1	7.7
6	8.6	9.0
7	10.2	10.6
8	12.4	12.6
9	15.7	15.5
10	31.2	27.1
All deciles	100.0	100.0
Top 1 percent	8.1	5.9

decile rises to 1.83 percent while the share of the top decile falls to 27.1 percent. This move toward equality may be partially obscured by the magnitude of the numbers involved. For example, while the increase in the share of income received by the lowest tenth of all families appears small, it constitutes a 24 percent increase in their income share. Consider alternatively what the income share of the bottom decile would be if taxes for households in that decile were zero, but the taxes on other households remained unchanged. Note that this would be as much as the tax system alone could possibly do to increase the share of income received by the poorest households, given the aggregate level of tax revenue. If families in the bottom decile paid no taxes, their share of total income would only be 2.07 percent, or 0.24 percentage points higher than their income share under the current tax system. Put in that perspective, the tax system raises the share of the bottom tenth of all households by about 60 percent of the maximum potential increase, given the overall tax burden. Of course, a proportional tax would not alter the income shares at all, so the changes in shares are another measure of the extent to which the actual tax system deviates in the direction of progressivity from a proportional tax on all income.

Note that the redistribution produced by the tax system does not stop with the bottom decile. As Table 9 shows, the tax system increases the shares of all but the top 20 percent of households. This property of redistribution is also implicit in Table 6 since all but the top two deciles of households pay less than the overall average rate of tax of 29.1 percent. As compared with a proportional tax rate at the average rate of 29.1 percent which would yield the same total revenues, the top fifth of households pay over $45 billion more in taxes under the actual tax system, while the bottom 80 percent of households pay less by the same amount. On a per household basis, the average family in the bottom 80 percent pays about $750 less in taxes while the average family in the top tenth pays about $6,000 more than it would with a proportional tax system.

Taxes and Net Transfers across the Income Distribution

While the tax system alone tends to equalize the distribution of income, the tax and transfer systems together are an even more powerful redistributive tool. To demonstrate the magnitude of the combined effects of these policies, Table 10 shows the average tax payments and net transfers received (that is, transfers less taxes) for households in each decile. As expected, the average dollar amount of tax payments rises sharply with household income from $353 for the average household among the lowest tenth to nearly seventy times that amount for the average family in the top decile. The net transfer

TABLE 10

TAXES AND NET TRANSFERS PER HOUSEHOLD

(dollars)

Income Decile	Average BTAT Income per Household	Average Tax Payment per Household	Average Net Transfer per Household
1	3,022	353	1,454
2	6,503	811	2,748
3	9,054	1,479	2,184
4	11,723	2,368	851
5	14,602	3,388	−693
6	17,664	4,501	−2,264
7	20,973	5,599	−3,624
8	25,579	7,183	−5,155
9	32,370	9,747	−7,628
10	64,138	24,624	−21,876
Top 1 percent	$166,037	$79,420	−$76,019

TABLE 11
Share of Total Tax Paid by Decile
(percent)

Income Decile	Sales and excise	Payroll	Income	Property and corporation income	Combined
1	0.7	0.8	0.1	1.0	0.6
2	1.6	2.0	0.6	1.7	1.4
3	3.0	3.8	1.3	2.5	2.5
4	4.7	6.3	2.7	3.2	3.9
5	6.6	9.1	4.5	3.7	5.6
6	8.6	11.6	6.9	4.3	7.5
7	10.6	13.5	9.6	5.0	9.4
8	13.1	15.7	13.3	6.5	11.9
9	16.9	18.2	19.1	10.6	16.2
10	34.2	19.0	42.0	61.5	40.9
All deciles	100.0	100.0	100.0	100.0	100.0

Type of Tax spans the Sales and excise, Payroll, Income, and Property and corporation income columns.

to households in the bottom fifth of the population averages about $2,000 while families in the top fifth pay about $15,000 more in taxes than they receive in transfers.

Distribution of the Overall Tax Burden

The share of the total tax burden borne by each income class can also be calculated. In Table 11, the share of the total burden borne by each decile of the population is displayed for each of the four major groups of taxes and for the overall tax system. In other words, the table shows the fraction of total revenue from each tax derived from households in each decile.

Obviously, for all taxes, households in the higher deciles pay a greater share of the total tax revenue. With a proportional tax system, each share would be equal to the decile's share of total income. For progressive taxes, both the rates faced by higher-income households and income upon which those rates are applied are greater so that shares of tax burden exceed shares of income. The top 15 percent of households pay approximately half of all taxes in the United States while the top decile alone contributes more than 40 percent of total tax receipts. In contrast, the bottom decile pays less than 1 percent, and the lower half of the population pays less than 15 percent of all taxes. The distribution of tax payments by decile is more unequal than the distribution of tax rates since the tax burden on a household is a product of its income and the average tax rate it faces.

Comparison of the distribution of taxes paid for the separate categories of taxes indicates that payroll taxes are spread most evenly across the population, while income taxes and taxes on capital income are borne most unevenly. The top decile pays over 60 percent of all capital taxes, and the top half of the income distribution bears over 90 percent of the income tax burden.

Tax Rates with Before-Tax, Before-Transfer Ranking

In the estimates presented earlier, households were ranked in the income distribution on the basis of their before-tax, after-transfer (BTAT) incomes. Since transfers are considered to be income by generally accepted definitions, this method of ranking is logical and has been employed in most studies of tax incidence and income distribution. It may be of some interest, however, to consider how the results would differ if households were ranked in the income distribution according to their before-tax, before-transfer (BTBT) incomes. In other words, the total income of households will be measured exactly as before (including transfers), but the position of households in the income distribution will be determined by factor earnings (labor plus capital income only).

Table 12 presents the average tax rates by type of tax for deciles when households are ranked in this way. While tax rates are higher for the top eight deciles than those shown in Table 6 where BTAT ranking is used, the differences are only modest. Tax rates are sharply lower, however, for the bottom two deciles. The total tax burden is only 3.0 percent of total income for the lowest decile and 7.2 percent for the second decile compared with rates of 11.7 and 12.5 percent for the first and second deciles under the conventional BTAT ranking. It should be emphasized that each individual household's tax burden, total income, and overall tax rate is exactly the same in Tables 12 and 6. The differences in these estimates are due solely to the fact that some households occupy different deciles in Table 12 than in Table 6.

An example will help clarify why the estimates in Tables 12 and 6 differ so greatly for the lowest deciles. Consider two households, A and B. Household A has no income except a government

TABLE 12
Average Tax Rates by Decile (BTBT Income)
(percent)

BTBT Income Decile	Type of Tax				
	Sales and excise	Payroll	Income	Property and corporation income	Combined
1	0.4	0.2	0.1	2.4	3.0
2	1.1	1.1	0.9	4.1	7.2
3	3.2	4.4	2.3	7.0	16.8
4	4.4	7.0	4.2	5.9	21.6
5	4.9	8.4	6.6	4.6	24.4
6	5.2	9.0	8.3	4.0	26.5
7	5.4	8.8	9.7	3.8	27.7
8	5.4	8.3	11.0	4.2	28.9
9	5.5	7.6	12.6	4.9	30.6
10	5.5	4.0	13.9	15.1	38.5
Top 1 percent	5.6	1.2	12.5	28.6	47.9
All deciles	4.9	6.2	10.0	7.9	29.1

transfer of $4,000 and bears a zero tax burden. Household B has no income except labor earnings of $3,000 and bears a tax burden equal to 15 percent of its labor income. When households are ranked on the basis of their BTAT incomes, household A is ranked above household B. With this ranking, the higher-income household has a lower tax rate than the lower-income household. Thus, when the conventional BTAT ranking is used, some relatively high-income households are subject to very low tax rates because they receive large nontaxable government transfers.

When these two households are ranked by their BTBT incomes, household B is ranked above household A since B's factor earnings are $3,000 compared with zero for A. Under this ranking method, the household with the lower tax rate is ranked lower in the income distribution. As suggested by this example, ranking households according to BTBT income tends to reduce estimated tax rates at the bottom of the income distribution by assigning households with large transfers and low factor incomes (and hence low taxes) to lower positions in the distribution. Consequently, the tax rates shown for the lowest deciles are lower in Table 12 than in Table 6.

The conventional BTAT ranking tends to conceal the fact that a sizable number of households bear a very small tax burden because households with relatively large transfers are assigned to the upper deciles where their taxes are averaged with other households whose burdens are greater because their income takes the form of factor earnings. By contrast, the BTBT ranking of Table 12 assigns households with the lowest factor earnings (who generally have relatively large transfers) to the bottom deciles. The nontaxable status of the transfers results in very low estimated tax rates for these deciles. Since transfers are relatively unimportant in the higher deciles, there is little difference between the BTAT and BTBT rankings for upper-income groups.

Tax Burdens for Middle-Aged Households

One consequence of using annual data on household income is that the elderly and young households are disproportionately represented in the lower deciles. This occurs because the young and elderly tend to be at low points in their lifetime income cycles. These age groups, however, especially the elderly, are the recipients of unusually large transfers that are frequently not available to other low-income households. For example, the elderly receive nearly all the transfers under social security, Medicare, and Supplemental Security Income, which accounted for almost half of all transfers in 1976. Since the very low tax rates for the lower deciles largely result from the fact that most income in these deciles takes the form of nontaxed government transfers, it is possible that the tax rates are low not so much because these households are poor but because they contain a large share of the elderly or young.

In other words, do households that normally have low incomes throughout their lifetimes bear small tax burdens even during their middle years? This question ultimately raises the issue of relating tax burdens to income over longer periods than a year. Our data do not permit us to develop such estimates, but it is possible to estimate the tax rates for a subset of all households that does not contain either the elderly or the young. In this way, at least it can be determined whether the inclusion of age groups normally receiving large transfers tends to influence the overall decile tax rates for the entire sample. We believe this procedure is likely to give a better clue to the lifetime or normal tax rates for different income classes than considering all age groups together.

Table 13 gives the estimated tax rates for the set of all households with the head of household between the ages of thirty-five and fifty-five. Since these years tend to be the most productive for

TABLE 13
Average Tax Rates of Households
with 35–55-Year-Old Heads
(percent)

			Type of Tax		
Income Decile	Sales and excise	Payroll	Income	Property and corporation income	Combined
1	2.5	4.0	1.1	5.0	12.6
2	3.3	5.4	2.9	4.3	15.9
3	4.4	7.7	4.9	3.5	20.6
4	4.8	8.7	6.5	2.8	22.9
5	5.1	9.0	8.1	2.8	25.1
6	5.3	8.8	9.4	2.6	26.1
7	5.3	8.4	10.7	2.9	27.3
8	5.4	7.9	11.8	3.5	28.7
9	5.4	7.2	13.3	4.1	30.1
10	5.6	4.0	15.0	12.8	37.4
All deciles	5.2	6.8	11.2	6.1	29.3

most households, we would expect transfers to be less important sources of income than for the full sample of all households. Despite this expectation, the estimated tax rates in Table 13 are remarkably close to the tax rates estimated for the entire sample as shown in Table 6.

Note that the tax rates for the lowest decile and the top five deciles for household heads aged thirty-five to fifty-five years differ by less than one percentage point from the corresponding tax rates for the set of all households. The lowest decile among those thirty-five to fifty-five years old receives 56 percent of its income as government transfers, compared with 60 percent for the lowest decile of all households. This result suggests that the lowest-income households, even when they are ineligible for the large programs aimed at the elderly, are still able to receive substantial assistance under other government programs. The greatest differences between Tables 13 and 6 are for the second to the fifth deciles where the tax rates are from two to four percentage points higher for those thirty-five to fifty-five years old. These modest differences suggest that our conclusion that the tax system is sharply progressive does not result from considering all age groups together.

Federal, State, and Local Tax Burdens

The federal government collected 68 percent of the 1976 tax revenues allocated in this study. Personal income taxes and social security payroll taxes accounted for the bulk of this revenue. The corporation income tax, which was the federal government's second largest source of revenue until its yield was surpassed by that of the social security payroll tax about ten years ago, is the third largest revenue source. These three taxes together produce about 90 percent of total federal revenues.

Table 14, showing the tax rates by deciles for federal taxes alone, indicates that, as expected, the federal tax system is progressive. Federal taxes average 7.0 percent of total income for the lowest decile, with the overall tax rate rising steadily until it reaches 23.9 percent for the tenth decile. The regressivity in the social security payroll tax from the seventh to the tenth decile is more than offset by the progressivity of the personal and corporation income taxes.

Since state and local governments rely on a different mix of taxes, the distribution of tax burdens under state and local taxes is also of interest. Sales and property taxes are the major revenue sources for state and local governments, with sales taxes used primarily by state governments and property taxes used mainly by local

TABLE 14

Average Rates of Federal Taxes
(percent)

Income Decile	Type of Tax				
	Excise	Payroll	Income	Corporation income	Combined
1	0.7	3.3	0.6	2.4	7.0
2	0.8	3.9	1.6	1.9	8.1
3	1.0	5.4	2.6	2.0	11.1
4	1.2	6.9	4.0	1.9	14.2
5	1.5	8.0	5.5	1.8	16.7
6	1.5	8.5	6.9	1.7	18.6
7	1.6	8.2	8.1	1.7	19.5
8	1.6	7.9	9.1	1.8	20.4
9	1.6	7.2	10.2	2.4	21.4
10	1.7	3.8	11.6	6.8	23.9
All deciles	1.4	6.2	8.5	3.6	19.8

TABLE 15

Average Rates of State and Local Taxes
(percent)

Income Decile	Sales and excise	Income	Property and corporation income	Combined
		Type of Tax		
1	1.6	0.1	3.1	4.7
2	1.8	0.2	2.3	4.4
3	2.4	0.4	2.5	5.2
4	2.9	0.5	2.5	6.0
5	3.2	0.9	2.3	6.5
6	3.5	1.2	2.2	6.9
7	3.6	1.4	2.1	7.1
8	3.7	1.7	2.3	7.7
9	3.7	2.0	2.9	8.6
10	3.8	2.0	8.6	14.4
All deciles	3.5	1.5	4.3	9.3

governments. Personal income taxes have become increasingly important in recent years, but they are still of lesser importance than sales and property taxes.

Table 15 shows the state and local tax system to be progressive overall, with the average tax rate rising from 4.7 percent for the bottom decile to 14.4 percent for the highest decile. This finding differs from previous tax incidence studies that have found state and local taxes to be regressive or, at most, only slightly progressive. The source of this difference lies, of course, in the treatment of sales and excise taxes. Our analysis implies that these taxes are progressive, while earlier studies have allocated them according to consumption and thus estimated their incidence to be regressive.

Although it is widely believed that federal taxes on average are far more progressive than state and local taxes, a comparison of Tables 14 and 15 suggests only a moderate difference in the degree of progressivity. The tax rate of the top decile under the federal system is 3.4 times the tax rate of the lowest decile; the state and local tax system yields a multiple of 3.1 for the same deciles. Although this comparison of top and bottom decile tax rates seems to imply that the degree of progressivity is almost identical, it may be more meaningful to compare tax rates of various deciles to the overall average tax rates. Thus, the 4.7 percent tax rate of state and local taxes for the lowest decile is 51 percent of the overall average state and local tax rate of 9.3 percent, while for federal taxes the rate for the lowest decile is 35 percent of the overall rate. In other words, state and local tax systems place, on average, a heavier burden per dollar of total revenue on lower-income classes than does the federal tax system. Viewed in this way, the federal tax system is more progressive, but the difference is less pronounced than previously realized.

Recall that our figures for state and local taxes represent averages across all states and localities. Households residing in regions with relatively heavier taxes than the national average would tend to bear a larger burden than suggested by Table 15, while residents of regions with relatively low state and local taxes would bear lighter burdens.

Tax Rates by Sources of Income

Before-tax income derives from three sources: labor income, capital income, and government transfers. As emphasized in Chapter 2, tax burdens depend on the source of income as well as the level of income. In this section, we examine the tax rates applicable to income from different sources for the various income classes.

To estimate tax rates by sources of income, it is necessary to allocate the burden of each tax to the type of income which is correspondingly reduced by the tax. Our earlier analysis indicated the proper way to do this for all taxes except personal income taxes. As discussed, corporation income and property taxes fall on capital income; payroll taxes fall on labor income up to the ceiling on taxable earnings; and sales and excise taxes are equiproportionate levies on capital and labor income. We likewise assume that personal income taxes fall equally on labor and capital income. In other words, if a household's tax burden under personal income taxes is 10 percent of its combined capital and labor income, it is assumed that this tax burden is the result of a 10 percent tax on labor income and a 10 percent tax on capital income.[1] Since no taxes fall on government transfers, the tax rate on transfer income is zero.

---

[1] This assumption is probably not accurate. Personal income taxes generally treat capital income more favorably than labor income by excluding some types of capital income (such as imputed income from owner-occupied housing) from the tax base. Thus, in fact, the average rate of personal income taxes on labor income is probably somewhat higher than the rate on capital income. Consequently, our estimated tax rates for capital income are probably too high while the rates for labor income are too low. This bias is probably not significant except for the top decile where capital income is relatively more important.

TABLE 16
Tax Rates on Labor and Capital Income
(percent)

Income Decile	Average Tax Rate on Capital Income	Average Tax Rate on Labor Income
1	45.9	19.9
2	48.3	21.0
3	49.3	22.1
4	50.8	23.5
5	52.1	24.8
6	53.5	25.9
7	54.7	26.4
8	56.0	27.2
9	57.6	27.8
10	58.5	26.8
All deciles	56.1	26.6

Table 16 shows the calculated tax rates on labor and capital income. The average tax rate on labor income across all income classes is 26.6 percent, while the corresponding figure for capital income is 56.1 percent, more than twice as high. The tax rates for each type of income rise with the income decile. For labor income, the tax rate rises from 19.9 percent for the lowest decile to 26.8 percent for the highest decile. The progression in the tax rate on labor income is the result of two opposing factors. First, payroll taxes are proportionate levies up to a ceiling on taxable earnings; above the ceiling, the average tax rate of this tax declines. Second, personal income taxes are progressive levies on labor income throughout the income distribution. The progressivity of personal income taxes more than offsets the regressivity (above the earnings ceiling) of payroll taxes except at the highest decile where there is a slight decline in the rate.[2]

The tax rate on capital income also is higher for the upper-income classes, rising from 45.9 percent for the lowest decile to 58.5 percent for the highest decile. This progressivity is due entirely to personal income taxes since the corporation, property, and sales and

___

[2] We suspect that there would be no decrease in the tax rate on labor income for the top decile if the data permitted correction of the bias introduced by the assumption that personal income taxes fall at the same rate on labor and capital income (see Chapter 4, note 1).

excise taxes are proportionate levies on capital income regardless of the total incomes of the households.

Tax rates on labor and capital incomes tend to be less progressive than tax rates on total income (as shown in Table 6). The very low tax rates on the total incomes of low-income households do not arise because of light taxation of their labor and capital incomes but because of the large proportion of their total incomes that take the form of untaxed transfers. A household that has a low factor income and receives no government transfers can bear a significant tax burden. For example, a household with no transfers but with factor earnings placing it in the lowest decile would be subject to a tax rate of about 25.2 percent, if labor income is assumed to be 80 percent and capital income 20 percent of its total income. Of course, such households must be relatively rare since transfers compose 60 percent of total income in the lowest decile.

In contrast to our earlier conclusions regarding tax rates on total income, the tax rates on labor and capital income are sensitive to the incidence assumptions employed. If part of the corporation and property taxes, for example, are assumed to be shifted to consumers (and hence become equiproportionate levies on labor and capital income), the estimated tax rates on capital income would be reduced and the estimated tax rates on labor income would be increased.

Marginal Tax Rates by Income Class

To this point the analysis has been concerned with the level of average tax rates, that is, total tax burdens as a percentage of total incomes. The data used here also permit estimation of the marginal tax rates confronting households at different income levels. Marginal tax rates are the rates that apply to a change in income. They indicate how much disposable income will change in response to a given change in before-tax earnings. For example, if a person's disposable income rises by only $60 when he earns an additional $100, the marginal tax rate is 40 percent; the government receives $40 in additional net revenue. Similarly, if a person's disposable income falls by only $30 when he earns $100 less, the marginal tax rate is 70 percent; the government receives $70 less in net revenue. A household's marginal tax rate will generally not be equal to its average tax rate.

Marginal tax rates on factor earnings are a product both of the tax system and of government transfers. Obviously, when a person increases his earnings, part of the increase goes to pay income taxes, sales taxes, social security taxes, and so on; his disposable income rises less than his earnings because of taxes. In addition, for many households, government transfer programs also produce implicit marginal tax rates by reducing the amount of the transfer received when earnings increase. For example, suppose that a person's transfer is reduced by $50 when he earns an additional $100; as a result, his disposable income rises by only $50—the same effect as a tax of 50 percent on the additional $100 in earnings. Since many government transfer programs are of this type, marginal tax rates for transfer recipients (generally low-income households) are often sizable.

Marginal tax rates are more important than average tax rates for a different type of analysis. The structure of average rates determines the distributional effects of the tax system: a progressive rate structure implies that the distribution of after-tax income is more nearly equal than the distribution of before-tax income. In contrast, marginal tax rates are important tools in estimating the effect of taxes and transfers on economic incentives: the higher the marginal tax rates, the lower the financial incentive to earn more income. Moreover, it is clear that the relevant measure of marginal tax rates is the effective rate that reflects the combined effect of the increase in taxes and the fall in transfers when earnings rise. If a person's transfer falls by $40 and his taxes rise by $20 when he earns an extra $100, his effective marginal tax rate is 60 percent.

Our method of estimating marginal tax rates is to relate average factor earnings (BTBT income) for each income class to its average disposable income (ATAT income) and then to use the change in moving from one income class to another to calculate the marginal tax rate for that interval. For example, suppose the average BTBT income in the sixth decile is $10,000 and average ATAT income is $8,000, compared with an average BTBT income of $15,000 and average ATAT income of $11,000 in the seventh decile. Since factor earnings rise by $5,000 in moving from the sixth to the seventh decile while disposable income rises by $3,000, we would calculate a marginal tax rate of 40 percent for this income interval. (The BTBT ranking is used for these calculations since the relevant concern is the variation of disposable income with a change in factor earnings.)

Marginal tax rates estimated by this procedure must be interpreted with some caution. There is likely to be considerable variation in the marginal tax rates of different households within each income class, and our estimates pertain only to the average household. In addition, there may be other biases in our procedure. For example, taxes and transfers vary with household characteristics other than income, and we have not controlled for these variables. Smaller-sized households, for instance, receive smaller transfers and pay higher taxes, other things being equal. Thus, the fact that average household size rises as income increases tends to impart a downward bias to our estimates of marginal tax rates. Similarly, social security transfers are received primarily by the elderly, who are disproportionately represented in the lower deciles. This may impart an upward bias to our estimates. While we believe there is no significant bias on the average, a disaggregated approach could be used to provide better estimates for selected population subgroups.

Table 17 presents estimates of effective marginal tax rates, as well as the marginal tax rates relating to the tax and transfer systems separately, for eight income classes. At the bottom, marginal tax rates are slightly above 60 percent for approximately the lowest third of all households while they are 46 percent for the interval from the ninth to the tenth deciles. Apparently, marginal tax rates are close to or above 50 percent for about half of all households. To estimate a "typical" marginal tax rate representing an average for all households, note that while average factor earnings rise by $61,015 in moving from the lowest- to the highest-income class, disposable income rises by only $33,247. This ratio implies an average marginal tax rate of 45.5 percent over the entire interval. Of course, as Table 17 shows, there is considerable variation around this average figure.

Marginal tax rates are high at low-income levels primarily because government transfers are large. Note that in the lowest income interval the transfer system contributes 35.3 percentage points of the 62.9 percent effective marginal tax rate. The high marginal tax rate for the highest-income class is almost entirely the result of the tax system. Effective marginal tax rates are lowest for the upper-middle-income classes. These classes, it should be noted, will be the most strongly affected by the 1977 changes in the social security payroll tax that sharply increased the ceiling on taxable earnings. When this change becomes effective, marginal tax rates will become significantly higher for the income classes that, in 1976, had the lowest marginal tax rates.

It must be emphasized that these estimates provide no clue as to how much productive incentives may have been impaired by high marginal tax rates on factor earnings. These rates indicate only the level of the financial incentive to alter factor earnings, not the nature of the response to these incentives.

TABLE 17
Marginal Tax Rates

	Average Amounts (dollars)				Marginal Tax Rate (percent)		
Decile	BTBT Income	Transfer	Tax	ATAT Income	Transfer system	Tax system	Effective combined rate
1+2	903	5,292	366	5,842			
					35.3	27.4	62.9
3	4,968	3,859	1,478	7,351			
					35.5	25.4	61.0
4	8,725	2,525	2,433	8,817			
					19.2	29.2	48.4
5	11,996	1,897	3,389	10,504			
					7.7	31.3	39.0
6	16,091	1,582	4,671	13,003			
					9.4	31.9	41.3
7	19,413	1,268	5,730	14,953			
					−0.3	34.4	34.1
8	23,901	1,282	7,273	17,909			
					0.2	36.4	36.6
9	30,729	1,268	9,759	22,239			
					−1.5	47.4	46.0
10	61,918	1,726	22,724	39,089			

APPENDIX

Accounting for the Uses Side
in Estimating Tax Burdens

The results reported in Chapter 4 differ in only one important respect from estimates developed in most other studies: taxes judged to fall on consumption in previous studies are allocated in proportion to factor income rather than consumption. The theoretical basis for this change in procedure was explained in Chapter 2. Two theoretical reasons were identified which, taken together, imply that allocation of sales and excise taxes to factor income is the correct approach. First, the real value of transfers is assumed to be unaffected by tax policy. Second, consumption-saving differences among income classes are small enough to be ignored when consumption out of normal, or permanent, income is considered.

These two arguments are theoretically separate. It is possible that real transfers should be kept constant while consumption-saving differences based on annual statistics should be taken into account. In this Appendix we consider the quantitative importance of these two issues, and compare alternative methods of allocating taxes which relax the assumptions of Chapter 2. In particular, when our procedure is adjusted to incorporate tax effects on the uses side of household budgets, we find that the overall tax system is more progressive than when these effects are ignored.

Sales and Excise Taxes

To incorporate considerations relating to the uses side of the budget, we need information on the consumption behavior of households which our data base does not include. We have, therefore, estimated consumption by utilizing the ratios of consumption to before-tax income for each decile that are implicit in the Pechman and Okner tax incidence study.[1] Since the Pechman-Okner study pertained to the year 1966, these estimates applied to 1976 data are probably somewhat inexact, but the general pattern of the relationships is likely to be similar enough for our purposes.

Column (1) of Table 18 presents these data in the form of saving as a percentage of disposable income. (Saving is equal, of course, to disposable income minus consumption.) The differences among income classes are quite pronounced. Households in the lowest decile average negative savings equal to 48.5 percent of disposable income; put differently, consumption of these households is equal to 148.5 percent of disposable income. The fraction of income saved rises steadily as income rises, reaching 34.4 percent for the top decile. Overall, the national average of disposable income saved is 13.4 percent.

Expressed relative to before-tax income, the lowest quintile consumes 131 percent of before-tax income while the highest quintile consumes only 40.5 percent. Consumption relative to income thus falls sharply as income increases; it is this characteristic of consumption-saving behavior that results in regressive tax rates for any tax allocated in proportion to consumption. This regressive quality is illustrated in column (2), where sales and excise taxes are allocated in proportion to consumption. By this calculation, the average tax rate for the lowest decile is more than three times greater than the average rate for the highest decile.[2] Column (4) shows the progressive pattern of tax rates when sales and excise taxes are allocated in proportion to factor income, the approach advocated in this study. The differences in rates shown in columns (2) and (4) largely account for the way our estimates of the overall incidence of the tax system differs from previous studies, at least under competitive incidence assumptions.

Now consider the issue of how sales and excise taxes affect government transfers. Allocation in proportion to consumption im-

---

[1] Joseph A. Pechman and Benjamin A. Okner, *Who Bears the Tax Burden?* (Washington, D.C.: Brookings Institution, 1974). Pechman and Okner do not report these ratios explicitly, but they can be computed by dividing sales and excise taxes as a percent of income (table 4-9, p. 61) by sales and excise taxes as a percent of consumption (table 5-8, p. 81).

[2] This calculation probably overstates the regressivity of these taxes under this approach because we have allocated excise taxes in proportion to total consumption rather than to consumption of the taxed items. If allocated to the taxed items, they would be less regressive since expenditure on these items is a lower percentage of total consumption for low-income classes (see Table 1). Pechman and Okner estimate tax rates for sales and excise taxes that range from 8.9 percent for the lowest decile to 3.2 percent for the highest.

TABLE 18
SALES AND EXCISE TAX BURDENS ADJUSTED FOR USES SIDE
(percent)

| | | Taxes Allocated According to | | | | |
| | Percentage of Disposable Income Saved | Consumption | Consumption minus transfers | Factor income (sources) | Uses Adjustment | Tax Rates with Sources + Uses Effects |
Income Decile	(1)	(2)	(3)	(4)	(5)	(6)
1	−48.5	10.6	7.3	2.3	5.0	7.3
2	−15.4	8.2	4.7	2.6	2.3	4.9
3	−1.0	6.8	4.5	3.4	1.2	4.6
4	1.3	6.4	5.2	4.1	1.0	5.1
5	3.1	6.0	5.7	4.7	0.9	5.6
6	4.9	5.7	5.9	5.0	0.7	5.7
7	8.4	5.4	5.9	5.2	0.4	5.6
8	11.1	5.2	5.7	5.3	0.2	5.5
9	14.0	4.9	5.5	5.3	0.0	5.3
10	34.4	3.3	3.7	5.5	−1.7	3.8
All deciles	13.4	4.9	4.9	4.9	0.0	4.9

plicitly assumes that the real value of transfers falls. One way of holding real transfers constant, while still taking into account differential saving-consumption behavior, is to proceed as follows: for each income class, subtract from total consumption the value of transfers received to arrive at consumption net of transfers. Then sales and excise taxes are allocated in proportion to net consumption (consumption not financed by transfers). In this way none of the tax burden is allocated to transfer income. The results of these calculations are shown in column (3). Tax burdens estimated in this way are noticeably less regressive than in the case where taxes are allocated to all consumption (including that financed by transfers), as in column (2). Indeed, except for the lowest and highest deciles, the tax rates are almost proportional.

The estimates in columns (2), (3), and (4) show the relative quantitative importance of the two theoretical arguments we have advanced to justify allocation of taxes in proportion to factor income. Moving from column (2) to column (3) shows the effect of keeping real transfers constant but still taking into account differences in consumption-saving ratios. Comparing column (4) to column (3) shows the additional effect produced when consumption-saving differences are ignored. Roughly speaking, the estimates in column (3) stand about midway between those in columns (2) and (4). Therefore, the assumption that real transfers are unaffected by tax policy accounts for about half the difference between our estimates and those of previous studies, while the assumption that consumption-saving differences can be ignored accounts for the remainder.

In Chapter 2 we presented the case to be made for the assumption that tax policy does not affect the real value of transfers; that analysis need not be repeated here. However, the quantitative significance of consumption-saving differentials for the analysis of tax incidence may bear further examination.

Our estimates of tax burdens identify the tax burdens on the sources side of household budgets. In the present context, burdens on the uses side of the budget stem from the effect on households of tax-induced changes in the relative costs of consumption and saving. If households across the income distribution differ in their consumption-saving ratios, these differences will affect the distribution of the tax burden. As explained in Chapter 2, the total tax burden on any household or income class is the sum of the effects on the sources and uses sides of budgets. Consequently, it is only necessary to calculate the effects on the uses side and add them to the figures in column (4) to adjust our estimates to take into account consumption-saving differences.

The effect of a tax on the uses side, expressed as a percentage of income, is the weighted average of the change in relative prices. The tax effect on the uses side can be calculated from the expression $a_i P_c^* + (1 - a_i) P_s^*$, as explained in Chapter 2. The terms a_i and $(1 - a_i)$, the weights for household i, are the percentages of income consumed and saved, while the terms P_c^* and P_s^* are the fractional changes in the prices of consumption and saving produced by the tax. (The "price" of saving can best be conceptualized as the present cost of future consumption. For example, a reduction in the net interest rate increases the present cost of future consumption since more must be saved at a lower rate to finance a given level of future consumption.) Column (1) in Table 18 gives the term $(1 - a_i)$ for each decile, so it is only necessary to estimate P_c^* and P_s^* to make the uses side adjustments.

Since sales and excise tax revenue equals 8.1 percent of total consumption, these taxes are assumed to increase the price of consumption relative to saving by this percentage. Hence, if units are defined so that initial prices are unity, $P_c^* - P_s^* = 0.081$. Moreover, since there is no net effect on the uses side for the community as a whole (the net burden on the sources side equals the tax revenue raised), $0.866P_c^* + 0.134P_s^* = 0$. (The national average percentages consumed and saved are 86.6 and 13.4. Only when households deviate from these average figures is there a nonzero net effect on the uses side from the change in relative prices.) These two equations allow us to solve for the two unknowns: $P_c^* = +0.011$ and $P_s^* = -0.07$.

Based on these figures, estimates of the uses-side effects of sales and excise taxes are presented in column (5) of Table 18. Note that households in the lowest eight deciles bear a net burden on the uses side. This occurs because these income classes consume more than 86.6 percent of their incomes (the national average), and the relative price of consumption has risen. Households in the highest decile benefit from the change in relative prices since they consume substantially below the average figure of 86.6 percent of income. (Ninth decile households also benefit slightly, but because of rounding the tax rate is entered as 0.0.) The combined uses effects for all deciles taken together is, of course, zero.

For each decile, summing the tax burdens from the sources and uses sides—columns (4) and (5)—yields the net tax rates shown in column (6). This calculation shows how the effects of changes in relative prices (effects on the uses side) can be incorporated into our framework while holding real transfers constant. Note that the estimates in columns (6) and (3) are virtually identical.[3] They simply represent alternative ways of arriving at the same net effects: in both cases, real transfers are assumed constant and differences in consumption-saving ratios are taken into account. The procedure involving separate estimation of sources and uses rates and summing them to obtain the net effect is the more general approach since it can be applied for any tax, not just for sales and excise taxes. The approach embodied in column (3) yields the correct estimates only because sales and excise taxes are assumed to be "neutral" on the sources side (that is, they affect labor and capital income proportionately), so that any deviations from the national average tax rate result from differences on the uses side. Some taxes, such as those on capital income, are not neutral on the sources side. In these cases, separate estimation of sources and uses effects is the most direct way to estimate net tax burdens.

---

[3] Small differences remain, presumably because of minor data inaccuracies and errors from rounding.

Our contention in Chapter 2 was that results are more reliable when the uses-side effects are ignored and tax burdens allocated on the sources side alone, as in column (4). This position primarily reflects two arguments. First, if uses adjustments are to be made, they must be made for all taxes that affect relative product prices and not just for sales and excise taxes. Second, and more important, consumption-saving differences among income classes are much less pronounced if periods longer than a year are considered; adjustments based on annual data, as in Table 18, column (6), greatly overstate the magnitude of effects from the uses side. The quantitative importance of these two considerations are examined in the next two sections.

Uses Effects of Other Taxes

Taxes that fall on capital income place a tax burden on the sources side to the extent that income takes the form of earnings from capital. These taxes, however, also affect the uses side since they reduce the net return from saving. This reduction implies a change in relative prices that favors consumption at the expense of saving, exactly opposite to the uses-side effects of taxes falling on consumption. In other words, even if a household has no current income from capital and, hence, no tax burden on the sources side, it will still bear a burden if it saves a larger than average portion of its income since this saving will purchase a smaller quantity of goods in the future.

Under competitive conditions, the corporation and property taxes fall on capital income. On the sources side, these taxes should be allocated in proportion to before-tax capital income. This procedure has been employed in this and most other recent studies. No study, however, has made an adjustment for the uses-side effect of these taxes, although the theoretical analysis supporting such an adjustment has been familiar for years.[4] It appears to be inconsistent to incorporate the uses-side effects of sales and excise taxes resulting from differences in the consumption-saving decision in different income classes and then fail to do so for corporation and property taxes. Consistency requires incorporating the uses effects of all taxes that have such effects, or, alternatively, ignoring the uses effects of all taxes. The latter approach has been the one adopted in previous chapters in this study, and the case to be made for this approach will be considered further in the next section. We will consider now,

---

[4] See Richard A. Musgrave, *The Theory of Public Finance* (New York: McGraw-Hill, 1959), pp. 374-382.

however, how the uses effects of corporation and property taxes can be estimated.

Corporate and property tax revenues were $124.3 billion in 1976, while before-tax capital income is estimated to be $319.8 billion. Thus, the effective tax rate imposed on capital income by these taxes is 38.9 percent. This taxation of capital income means that the cost of saving (consuming in the future) is increased substantially relative to the cost of consuming now; consequently, the uses adjustment will favor those who consume a percentage of their income greater than the national average. The effects of the uses-side adjustments for corporate and property taxes, made using the consumption-saving fractions reported in column (1) of Table 18, are shown in Table 19.

Column (1) of Table 19 shows the tax rates on the sources side for corporate and property taxes under competitive assumptions. Column (2) gives the tax rates implied by the uses-side adjustment for each decile. Households in the lower-income classes actually gain (enjoy a negative tax rate) on the uses side because they devote very high percentages of their incomes to consumption, the relative price of which is decreased. On the other hand, households in the highest decile bear a large additional burden on the uses side because they save 34.4 percent of their income, far above the national average of

TABLE 19

CORPORATE AND PROPERTY TAX BURDENS ADJUSTED FOR USES SIDE
(percent)

	Competitive Assumptions			Noncompetitive Assumptions		
Income Decile	Sources (1)	Uses (2)	Total (3)	Sources (4)	Uses (5)	Total (6)
1	5.5	−24.0	−18.5	4.5	−10.2	−5.7
2	4.2	−11.2	− 7.0	4.1	− 4.7	−0.6
3	4.5	− 5.6	− 1.1	4.9	− 2.3	2.6
4	4.4	− 4.7	− 0.3	5.5	− 2.0	3.5
5	4.1	− 4.0	0.1	5.7	− 1.7	4.0
6	3.9	− 3.2	0.7	5.9	− 1.4	4.5
7	3.8	− 2.0	1.8	5.9	− 0.8	5.1
8	4.1	− 0.9	3.2	6.1	− 0.4	5.7
9	5.3	0.2	5.5	6.8	0.1	6.9
10	15.4	8.2	23.6	12.2	3.5	15.7
All deciles	7.9	0.0	7.9	7.9	0.0	7.9

13.4 percent, and the relative cost of saving is increased by corporate and property taxes. Column (4) gives for each decile the effective rate, the sum of the rates shown in columns (1) and (2). As a result of including the uses-side effects, the incidence of corporate and property taxes becomes much more progressive.

Under the noncompetitive incidence assumptions described in Chapter 2, half of corporate and property taxes are assumed to have the same incidence as sales and excise taxes. On the sources side, this portion of the taxes is allocated in proportion to factor income. On the uses side, this portion of the taxes works to the disadvantage of those who consume a large proportion of their incomes. The remaining portion of corporate and property taxes, however, still favors those who consume a heavier than average proportion of their income. On balance, the uses-side adjustment depends on whether capital income or consumption is more heavily taxed. Since half of corporate and property tax revenues equals $62.15 billion, or 6.4 percent of total consumption, while the remaining half equals 22.8 percent of before-tax capital income,[5] the net effect is to change relative prices in favor of consumption.

Columns (4), (5), and (6) of Table 19 give the sources, uses, and total tax rates under the specified noncompetitive conditions. The result of adding the uses-side effects to the tax rates on the sources side is once more to make these taxes more progressive, though to a significantly lesser degree than under competitive conditions.

Therefore, incorporating the uses-side effects of taxes makes sales and excise taxes less progressive than our original estimates while making corporate and property taxes more progressive. Other taxes may also have relative price effects. For example, personal income taxes fall on some types of capital income, but at the same time several special provisions in the tax laws are designed to favor saving. On balance, it is not clear whether this tax favors saving relative to consumption or the reverse. Payroll taxes, on the other hand, presumably have no effects on relative prices. In the estimates discussed below, we assume that personal income and payroll taxes are neutral on the uses side, although we recognize that this assumption may be questioned in the case of personal income taxes.

Table 20 brings together the results of calculations in this and the previous section. It shows the estimated tax rates, with uses-side

---

[5] Note that the tax rate on capital income does not fall by 50 percent because before-tax capital income is smaller in the noncompetitive case. In the competitive case, it is assumed that all the revenue of these taxes would have been capital income in the absence of the taxes, but in the noncompetitive case some of this revenue would have accrued to labor income.

TABLE 20
OVERALL TAX BURDENS ADJUSTED FOR USES SIDE
(percent)

Income Decile	Competitive Assumptions					Noncompetitive Assumptions				
	Sales and excise (1)	Corporate and property (2)	Payroll and income (3)	Total (4)	Sources only (5)	Sales and excise (6)	Corporate and property (7)	Payroll and income (8)	Total (9)	Sources only (10)
1	7.3	−18.5	4.0	−7.2	11.7	7.3	−5.7	4.0	5.6	10.8
2	4.9	− 7.0	5.7	3.6	12.5	4.9	−0.6	5.7	10.0	12.4
3	4.6	− 1.1	8.4	11.9	16.3	4.6	2.6	8.4	15.6	16.7
4	5.1	− 0.3	11.6	16.4	20.2	5.1	3.5	11.6	20.2	21.2
5	5.6	0.1	14.4	20.1	23.2	5.6	4.0	14.4	24.0	24.7
6	5.7	0.7	16.6	23.0	25.5	5.7	4.5	16.6	26.8	27.3
7	5.6	1.8	17.7	25.1	26.7	5.6	5.1	17.7	28.4	28.6
8	5.5	3.2	18.7	27.4	28.1	5.5	5.7	18.7	29.9	29.8
9	5.3	5.5	19.4	30.2	30.0	5.3	6.9	19.4	31.6	31.4
10	3.8	23.6	17.4	44.8	38.3	3.8	15.7	17.4	36.9	35.5
All deciles	4.9	7.9	16.2	29.1	29.1	4.9	7.9	16.2	29.1	29.1

adjustments included, for the major categories of taxes in columns (1), (2), and (3), under the assumption of competitive conditions. Column (4) shows the effective, or combined, tax rate of the entire tax system for each decile. For purposes of contrast, column (5) shows the effective tax rates when the uses-side adjustments are not made. Note that including the uses-side effects makes the overall tax system substantially more progressive, reducing significantly the estimated tax burden of the lowest decile and increasing the burden for the highest decile. This increase in progressivity occurs because sales and excise taxes penalize consumption far less than corporate and property taxes penalize saving.

Columns (6) through (10) present the results for the case of non-competitive assumptions for the corporate and property taxes.[6] Here, including the uses-side effects also makes the tax system more progressive, although to a lesser extent than in the competitive case. Indeed, except for the lowest two deciles, the effective tax rates are little changed by inclusion of the uses-side effects. The small changes in the effective rates are, however, the result of significant but opposing changes in the estimated rates of sales and excise taxes, which become less progressive, and corporate and property taxes, which become more progressive.

Significance of Consumption-Saving Differences

The magnitudes of the uses-side adjustments developed in the two previous sections are greatly influenced by the wide disparities in average saving rates reported in Table 18. These saving rates are estimated from surveys of households that attempt to measure consumption and income during a single year. Apart from possible inaccuracies in data collected in this way,[7] it is clear that these saving rates are strongly affected by the use of a one-year accounting period. This effect of the accounting period is obvious for the lowest decile, which is estimated to consume 148.5 percent of disposable income. It is possible for a household to consume more than its

---

[6] Because of computational difficulties, competitive assumptions are retained for the payroll tax, in contrast to the estimates in Table 8.

[7] Even granting the bias introduced by using a one-year accounting period, we are skeptical of these estimates. For the lowest decile, subtracting consumption accounted for by transfers still leaves consumption equal to about 250 percent of after-tax earnings. We find it difficult to understand how the average household in the poorest decile can finance that much consumption, even though we recognize that some nonpoor families with temporarily low incomes can do this. Misreporting of income, especially transfer income, is common in surveys, and the saving rates calculated for the lower deciles may be quite inaccurate.

income by drawing on its assets (for example, by financing consumption by withdrawals from a savings account) or borrowing, but this dissaving cannot continue for any extended period. Over a longer time no household can consume more than its disposable income if income and consumption are appropriately defined and measured.

In other words, people who have low incomes do not normally consume more than 100 percent of their disposable incomes. The 148.5 percent estimate of Table 18, if accurate, reflects the fact that in the survey year many families found themselves with temporarily depressed incomes and were therefore depleting their assets or borrowing to maintain their former (and expected future) standard of living. The important question is whether the consumption-saving behavior of families with temporarily changed circumstances should provide the basis for estimating how the tax system affects those with normally low or high incomes. Insofar as the concern in estimating the distribution of tax burdens is with the effect of the tax system on those who generally have low or moderate or high incomes, the relevant saving rates are those which reflect these households' normal behavior, not the abnormally low (or high) saving rates which occur when their incomes are unusually high (or low).

Of course, to estimate normal tax burdens accurately would require even more adjustments to our technique. For example, our tax rates are computed as tax burdens divided by annual income; for the lowest deciles annual income is less than permanent income and our tax rates are on this account biased upward. The reverse is true for the highest deciles. On the other hand, many of the taxes paid will be lower when annual income is low. The extent to which these effects are offsetting cannot be determined. Consequently, one should view the substitution of normal saving data for saving rates based on annual data as an attempt to correct just one of the more flagrant biases caused by using data derived from an arbitrary accounting period.

Unfortunately, there are no reliable estimates of the fraction of permanent income saved at different income levels. The permanent income hypothesis argues that saving is proportional to permanent income, which would require no uses-side adjustment to be made. Economists are far from agreeing on the validity of this hypothesis,[8] but there is wide agreement that annual saving data greatly overstate the differences among income classes. To illustrate the impact

---

[8] See Thomas Mayer, *Permanent Income, Wealth, and Consumption* (Berkeley and Los Angeles: University of California Press, 1972), for a survey and evaluation of the available evidence.

of a "reasonable" pattern of saving rates, we have estimated tax burdens using a hypothetical set of saving rates, shown in column (1) of Table 21. The saving rate is assumed to vary from 5 percent for the lowest decile to 19 percent for the highest. This assumed variation in saving behavior relative to permanent income is probably greater than many economists believe to be the case. It is plausible, however, that low-income households save less, in part because social security is likely to substitute more fully for private saving at low-income levels. Our purpose is not to argue that these rates are necessarily correct, but rather to show that the uses-side adjustments are small even when there are significant differences in saving rates.

Columns (2) and (3) of Table 21 show the distribution of tax burdens (sources plus uses) for sales and excise taxes and for corporate and property taxes under competitive incidence assumptions. These figures incorporate the uses-side adjustments based on the assumed saving rates. Column (4) gives the distribution of tax rates for all taxes together. This column should be compared with column (5), which reproduces our estimates for all taxes together based on sources-side effects only. As can be seen, the differences are quite small, exceeding one percentage point only for the bottom three and top deciles. Even when saving rates vary from 5 to 19 percent, the uses-side adjustments do not greatly affect the pattern of rates for all taxes taken together. This reflects in part the offsetting effects of the uses adjustment for sales and excise taxes, which make the tax rates less progressive, and the adjustment for corporate and property taxes, which makes them more progressive.

Columns (6) through (9) present the estimated tax rates for the noncompetitive incidence assumptions for the corporate and property taxes. As can be seen from comparing columns (8) and (9), the incorporation of uses-side effects produces a negligible change in estimated tax rates at all income levels.

The estimates in Table 21 suggest that the estimated tax rates on the sources side alone are reasonably accurate even when there are fairly sizable differences in saving rates. Incorporation of the uses-side effects does tend to make the tax system more progressive, but the magnitude of the change is significant only when implausibly large differences in saving rates are used. This outcome, of course, reflects the fact that the tax system, on balance, is biased against saving, even under fairly extreme noncompetitive assumptions. But, to repeat, the significance of this anti-saving tilt of the tax system for estimating tax rates by income class appears to be rather modest.

TABLE 21
Tax Burdens Incorporating
Uses-Side Adjustments with Hypothetical Saving Assumptions
(percent)

Income Decile	Percentage of Disposable Income Saved (1)	Competitive Assumptions				Noncompetitive Assumptions			
		Sales and excise (2)	Corporate and property (3)	All taxes (4)	Sources only (5)	Sales and excise (6)	Corporate and property (7)	All taxes (8)	Sources only (9)
1	5	2.9	2.3	9.1	11.7	2.9	3.1	10.0	10.8
2	5	3.2	1.0	9.9	12.5	3.2	2.7	11.6	12.4
3	5	4.0	1.3	13.7	16.3	4.0	3.5	15.9	16.7
4	10	4.4	3.1	19.2	20.2	4.4	4.9	20.9	21.2
5	10	5.0	2.8	22.2	23.2	5.0	5.1	24.4	24.7
6	10	5.3	2.6	24.5	25.5	5.3	5.3	27.0	27.3
7	10	5.5	2.5	25.7	26.7	5.5	5.3	28.3	28.6
8	15	5.1	4.8	28.6	28.1	5.1	6.3	29.8	28.6
9	15	5.1	6.0	30.5	30.0	5.1	7.0	31.4	29.8
10	19	5.1	17.6	40.1	38.3	5.1	13.1	36.0	35.5
All deciles	13.4	4.9	7.9	29.1	29.1	4.9	7.9	29.1	29.1

As mentioned in Chapter 2, we have no objection in principle to incorporating uses-side effects in the estimation of tax burdens, if performed consistently for all taxes, with normal spending behavior taken into consideration. In practice, however, we do not believe such adjustments can be made accurately enough at present to warrant their inclusion. There are several reasons for this belief. First, we have no reliable estimates of saving as related to normal income. Second, the theoretical methodology for making uses-side adjustments for an economy with positive saving is not adequately developed in the economics literature. The procedure we employed essentially applies the approach developed for estimating uses-side effects for an all-consumption economy to an economy with positive saving rates. The reliability of this approach requires further theoretical investigation. Third, all important uses-side effects should be incorporated. Their inclusion would involve determining the combined effect of all taxes on relative prices. In our calculations we have tried to assess the effects of sales, excise, corporate, and property taxes on the relative prices of consumption and saving, but other prices may be affected. In addition, other taxes, especially personal income taxes, may have effects on relative prices. On balance, it is clear that the effect of all taxes on relative prices is not known with any certainty.

In view of these factors, we believe that any uses-side adjustments that are made are likely to be highly inexact, so we prefer to allocate all taxes on the sources side. It should be emphasized once more that this procedure is quite accurate if spending patterns do not differ greatly among income classes because under these circumstances the uses-side adjustments are very small. Thus, the estimates of this study should prove to be fairly reliable, especially when the tax system as a whole is considered.